Capitals of the Caucasus

Stephen Stocks

CONTENTS

Capitals of the Caucasus

About this guide

This easy-to-use series of city guides helps you to unearth the treasures of the *Capitals of the Caucasus*. You will get in-depth information on all buildings, statues, parks, markets, places of worship and any other point of interest, researched through personal visits and by drawing on the expertise of locals. Every step of the way, uncluttered easy-to-follow maps guide you around the cities.

This book is organised into three sections, dedicated to Tbilisi, Yerevan and Baku respectively. Each of these are further organised into readily digestible chunks. You will find a brief history of each city and a precis of its history, geography and demographics. A series of leisurely walking tours have been designed so that you can take in all of the main sights without the hassle of tackling public transport or negotiating with taxi drivers. You will also discover the best day trips out of each city, and also get the essential practical information needed to make your trip plain sailing.

Welcome to the *Capitals of the Caucasus*!

TBILISI | *Georgia*

Tbilisi has an irresistible charm that is neither European nor Asian, but rather a unique blend of cultural influences concocted over centuries of turbulent history. Some boldly assert that Tbilisi acts, not just as the capital of Georgia, but also as a capital for the entire Caucasus region. Of course, proud Azeris and Armenians would dispute this vociferously.

The fact remains that, for centuries, first-time visitors to the Caucasus made a beeline for Tbilisi before exploring any other city. John Steinbeck, who documented his 1948 travels in Russia in *A Russian Journal*, remarked: "The magical name of Georgia came up constantly. Indeed, we began to believe that most Russians hope that if they live good and virtuous lives, they will not go to heaven but to Georgia when they die'.

At the centre of Georgian life, Tbilisi lives up to its billing. Its setting is nothing short of dramatic, arrayed along the banks of the swiftly-flowing Mtkvari river, under the brooding battlements of Narikala fortress and the green slopes of Mtatsminda Park. In the old town, houses crowd the higgledy-piggledy alleyways, their ornate balconies jutting out precariously in varying degrees of decay. Centuries of religious tolerance becomes apparent when you stumble upon ancient churches, mosques, synagogues and even a

Zoroastrian fire temple. Masseurs in sulphur bathhouses continue to scrub and pummel away, as they have done for centuries. Grand buildings line nineteenth-century boulevards, and everywhere the urban sprawl is broken up by leafy parks providing tired tourists with the chance to rest their weary feet. Neighbourhood bakeries and restaurants churn out endless supplies of khachapuri and khinkali, while cellars showcase their vintage Georgian wines.

Tbilisi offers an accessible, traveller-friendly infrastructure, with a wide selection of hotels and restaurants catering to every taste. Public transport stretches into every corner of the city, making it easy and cost-effective to see all the sights.

The city has come so far since Soviet times, and its development has accelerated even more after the Rose Revolution in 2003. The city is still not overrun with tourists, and many of the sights you'll have to yourself. And what's even better, the visa regime has been significantly relaxed, with many nationalities visa-exempt or eligible for e-visas. So now's the perfect time to visit, and this book will be your companion as you explore the city. Welcome to Tbilisi.

Contents

- *Getting to know Tbilisi* gives a brief history of the city and examines its history, geography and demographics.
- *Tbilisi Walking Tour 1* navigates north from Freedom Square and takes a walk up Tbilisi's grand thoroughfare, Rustaveli Avenue.
- *Tbilisi Walking Tour 2* wanders west of the Mtkvari river and explores the winding alleyways and ancient churches of Tbilisi's historical heart.
- *Tbilisi Walking Tour 3* steps south from Gorgasali Square to experience sulphur baths, hidden waterfalls and the lofty battlements of Narikala fortress.
- *Tbilisi Walking Tour 4* crosses the river to the experience the atmospheric nineteenth-century streets of the east bank.
- *Day Trips from Tbilisi* goes further afield to see the UNESCO World Heritage sights of Mtskheta and Gori, the birthplace of Stalin.
- *Preparing for your visit* gives you all the essential practical information needed to make your trip plain sailing.

* * *

List of Maps

- **Map A**: Freedom Square to Georgian National Parliament
- **Map B**: Georgian National Parliament to 9 April Park
- **Map C**: 9 April Park to Tbilisi Funicular and Mount Mtatsminda sights
- **Map D**: Rustaveli Theatre to Biltmore Hotel
- **Map E**: Georgian National Academy of Sciences to Rose Revolution Square
- **Map F**: Gorgasali Square to Erekle II Street
- **Map G**: Erekle II Street to Tbilisi Town Hall
- **Map H**: Tbilisi Town Hall to Lado Gudiashvili Square
- **Map I**: Lado Gudiashvili Square to Kote Afkhazi Street
- **Map J**: Gorgasali Square to Orbeliani Baths
- **Map K**: Orbeliani Baths to the Botanical Gardens
- **Map L**: Botanical Gardens to Aerial Tram and Rike Park
- **Map M**: Marjanishvili Square to Dry Bridge Market
- **Map N**: Dry Bridge Market to St Trinity Cathedral
- **Map O**: St Trinity Cathedral to Gorgasali Square

Getting to know Tbilisi

A brief history

The history of Tbilisi spans more than 1500 years and accordingly many myths swirl around its formation. The most popular of these describes how King Vakhtang Gorgasali was hunting in the woods along the banks of the Mtkvari river. He wounded a pheasant which subsequently dropped into one of the many hot springs in the area. The water had a miraculous curative effect, and the bird flew off to live another day. The king, amazed by the healing powers of the water, decided to move his capital here from Mtskheta forthwith. 'Tbili' in Georgian means warm, and so was an apt name for a settlement centred on so many hot springs.

It was the son of Vakhtang Gorgasali, King Dachi, who eventually succeeded in actually moving the capital to Tbilisi in the sixth century, and in building the all-important defences. However, the walls did not deter a procession of invading armies over the centuries, and by some accounts, there were forty separate conquests. Each time parts of Tbilisi were either destroyed or damaged and then renovated and rebuilt during intervening periods of peace. The result is a city with multiple layers of history, and many of the old buildings you see today are built on top, or from, much earlier structures.

From the sixth to the twelfth centuries, there were successive waves of Arab, Khazar, Seljuk Turk and Persian occupations. Then King David the Builder made his triumphal appearance, winning the city back and making it the capital once again of a united Georgia. He earnt his nickname from his ambitious renovation and construction projects throughout the city, and under his leadership, Tbilisi grew into a leading economic centre of the Caucasus. This was an enlightened golden age, during which the arts flourished, and Shota Rustaveli penned his most accomplished works.

Alas, as is the way in this part of the world, it did not last long, and darkness returned in the form of a crushing defeat at the hands of the Mongols in the thirteenth century. Turbulent times returned, and hostile forces repeatedly invaded the city. During the sixteenth to eighteenth centuries, the Persians and Turks generally held the upper hand, with the city experiencing great deprivations. It was not until 1748 that King Erekle II managed to drive the invaders out.

In the latter half of the eighteenth century, Georgia became the frontline of the Great Game between the Russia, Persian and Ottoman empires. Tbilisi had the unenviable task of deciding which power to support to secure its own best interests. Eventually, the rulers turned to Russia for support. However, this was not always forthcoming and invading Persians destroyed large segments of the city in 1795. Nevertheless, the country joined the Russian empire in 1800, signalling an end to the Royal family, and surrendering independence for the best part of two more centuries.

Under Russian rule, Tbilisi grew economically and politically. A significant amount of infrastructure was built, with new roads and railways connecting Tbilisi to other parts of the Caucasus and the Russian empire. New buildings were erected, and the city became a major cultural centre, with poets, artists and writers all coming to prominence during this time. At the turn of the century, Tbilisi played host to many anti-Tsarist revolutionaries, and it was here that Georgian Josef Stalin started out on his career. When the Tsarist regime eventually fell in 1918, Georgia declared independence, although a couple of years later was subsumed into the Soviet Union. Tbilisi and Georgia then waited another seventy years to feel the taste of freedom once more.

Geography

Tbilisi is Georgia's capital, situated in the southeast of the country. It is roughly equidistant from the borders with Azerbaijan and Armenia, both approximately forty to fifty kilometres away. The city is just above 41 degrees north and sits at an altitude of between 380 - 770 metres. Tbilisi is surrounded on three sides by various mountain ranges, and the Lori plain stretches away to the east.

The Mtkvari river dissects the city into two roughly equal parts. The oldest section is to the west of the river, and the dominant features here are the hills upon which the Narikala fortress and Mtatsminda Park are located. The main thoroughfare in this part of town is Rustaveli Avenue, lined by grand buildings of note. It links Freedom Square to Rose Revolution Square and the Vera and Vake neighbourhoods. The other side of the river is flatter and more regularly laid out. Here, Davit Aghmashenebli Avenue is the busiest street, lined with shops, restaurants and commerce of all types.

For most visitors, most sights of interest lie to the west of the river, although the eastern bank also has its highlights. The main tourist areas are bounded by the Botanical Gardens in the south, Vera Park in the north, Mtatsminda Park in the west, and St. Trinity Cathedral in the east.

Demographics

Just over 1.2 million people live in Tbilisi, which means that around a third of the entire Georgian population lives within its municipal limits. The city's population is likely to steadily rise over the coming decades as more people migrate to cities from the countryside. This growth contrasts with forecasts of a declining national population, primarily brought about by the economic situation putting downward pressure on family size.

While Tbilisi is overwhelmingly Georgian, the city still exudes a cosmopolitan atmosphere, with the biggest ethnic minorities, as you'd expect, being Russian, Azerbaijanis and Armenians. However, there are also Ukrainians, Greeks, Kurds, Yazidis and many others making up this melting pot.

The majority of people (84%) follow Georgian Orthodox Christianity. However, Georgia is famed for its long-held religious freedom and tolerance. Accordingly, you can find synagogues, mosques and a wide variety of churches serving Christian minorities.

Languages

Georgian is the official language, a Kartvelian tongue with a unique script, that is said to be one of the oldest languages still surviving today. It is spoken by 88% of citizens. The most popular second languages are Russian and English. You will probably find that older people are more likely to speak Georgian with quite fluent Russian, and youngsters will have a better grip of English. Interestingly, Georgian bears no resemblance to the languages of its neighbours, Azerbaijani and Armenian, and derives from an entirely different linguistic family.

Tbilisi Walking Tour 1 - Navigating north from Freedom Square

This walking tour begins at the very heart of Tbilisi, Freedom Square. Most hotels and other tourist accommodation should be within easy reach of this busy part of town. If you are staying a little further out, there is a red line metro station in the square. Many bus routes also stop here.

* * *

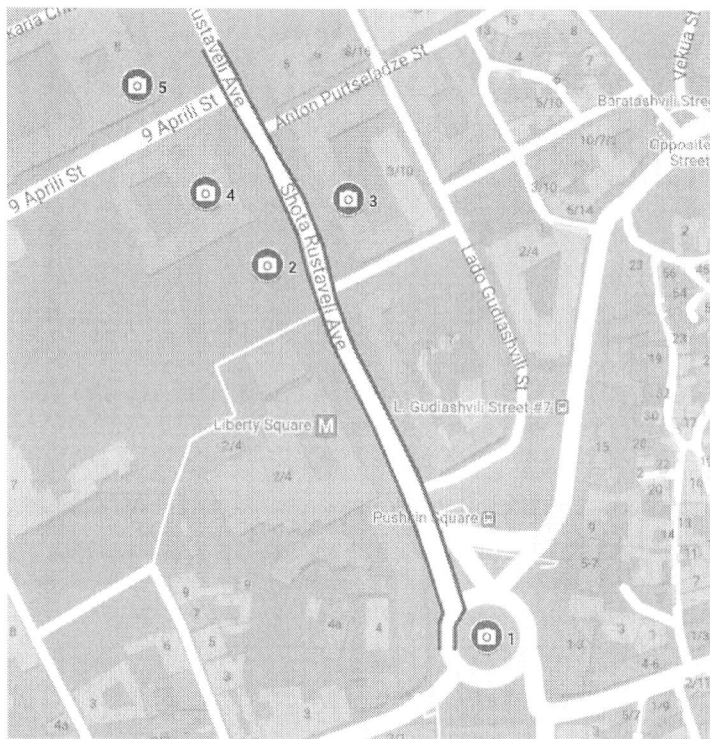

Map A: Freedom Square to Georgian National Parliament

Key:
  1. Freedom Square
  2. Garden of the First National Republic
  3. Georgia National Museum
  4. Viceroy's (Vorontsov's) Palace
  5. Georgian National Parliament

Freedom Square

Freedom Square *(Map A, Point 1)* dates back to the beginning of the nineteenth century, the time when the grand Rustaveli Avenue was also laid out. Its original name was Paskevich Square, honouring a victorious general of the Russian Empire. It was renamed Freedom Square when the country declared independence in 1918, although during most of the Soviet Union days it was referred to as Lenin Square.

The most prominent feature is a tall column at the top of which is a gilded statue of St. George on horseback. This is dedicated to the liberty and independence of the Georgian people and replaced a loathed Lenin monument that stood for years on the same spot.

Freedom Square has been the site of many national celebrations and also demonstrations; it's the focal point of the country. In an infamous incident in 2005, there was an attempted assassination attempt on US President George W Bush when a protestor threw a live hand grenade at the visiting leader. Thankfully, it failed to go off!

Garden of the First Republic of Georgia

As you walk up Rustaveli Avenue, on the left-hand side, look out for the wrought iron railings which form the elegant entrance to the Garden of the First Republic of Georgia *(Map A, Point 2)*. This private garden of the adjacent palace was the exclusive preserve of the elite.

The garden was extensively renovated and redesigned in the mid-eighteenth century by Swedish architect Ottom Jacob Simonson, and the layout you see today is mostly his work. He also added the grand staircase leading up to the shady terrace of the adjacent Vorontsov Palace (see below). Politicians signed the Independence Act in this palace in 1918, hence the name of the garden.

If you are a keen horticulturalist, there are some rare

species of plant to look out for here, including the red pine, Chinese flowering chestnut, bleeding heart and white fir.

Georgian National Museum

Opposite the Garden of the First Republic is the Georgian National History Museum *(Map A, Point 3)*. This early twentieth-century building incorporates classic Georgian medieval decorative elements. The museum traces its history back to 1852, when the Russian Imperial Geographical Society founded an institution to showcase historically significant items from across the Caucasus.

The first floor of the museum houses a collection of archaeological and ethnographical artefacts from the Neolithic, Bronze, Iron and Middle Ages. The second and third floors are dedicated to the Museum of Soviet Occupation (the main ticket price includes to the exhibit) and give a fascinating insight into this dark period of Georgia's history.

The museum is open from Tuesdays to Sundays from 10 am to 6 pm. The entrance fee is 7 GEL.

Viceroy's (or Vorontsov's) Palace

This palace was one of the very first buildings to have been built on Rustaveli Avenue, dating back to 1807, as the residence of the Russian Viceroy *(Map A, Point 4)*. The arcade, with its many impressive arches, was added later in the middle of the nineteenth century. At one time Stalin's mother lived here, although nowadays it is mainly used for youth activities.

Capitals of the Caucasus

It is often referred to as 'Vorontsov's Palace', honouring one of the more popular Russian Viceroys who oversaw a period of renaissance in Georgia, from 1844 to 1853. During his rule, he embarked upon many initiatives, founding theatres, libraries and museums, and restoring churches and historical monuments. He paid particular attention to education and the preservation of Georgian culture and made the teaching of Georgian compulsory. This commitment to local culture was even more remarkable considering that the official Russian policy was to further its way of life throughout the empire.

However, the history of this building does not end with the retirement of Vorontsov as Viceroy. In 1917, after the Russian Revolution and the collapse of the Russian Empire, the three Caucasian countries, Georgia, Armenia and Azerbaijan, rejected Lenin's new regime. The states instead formed their own Transcaucasian Federation, which met in the Vorontsov Palace throughout 1917. However, Georgians kept insisting on their national independence, and on 26 May 1918, they declared independence, prompting the collapse of the Federation. The Independence Act, which ushered in the first Georgian Republic, was signed here. Armenia and Azerbaijan also declared independence from here in the following days.

Georgian National Parliament

Next door to Vorontsov's Palace, a few steps further up Rustaveli Avenue, is the monumental former Georgian parliament building *(Map A, Point 5)*. Its role as the home to national legislators came to an abrupt end in 2012 when parliament was moved to a futuristic new home in Kutaisi, more than 200 km to the west. However, as all the ministries are still in Tbilisi, many MPs regard this separation as inefficient. So, who knows, maybe one day parliament might move back.

The parliament building was constructed between 1938 and 1953, partly with the help of German prisoners of war, and was initially designed to house the Georgian Soviet. Since independence, the building has witnessed some of the most critical events of recent modern Georgian history. On the 9 April 1989, Soviet Army troops forcibly broke up anti-Soviet demonstrations outside the parliament building, causing a stampede that killed twenty-one people. This event radicalised Georgian opposition to Soviet power. Then, in 1991 during the Georgian Civil War, government opposition fighters attacked the parliament building. Their action damaged the side wings of the structure and eventually forced the then-President Gamsakhurdia to flee to Armenia and then Chechnya, where he led a government-in-exile for the next eighteen months. Finally, in November 2003, the mass protests of the ultimately peaceful Rose Revolution, occurred in the streets around the parliament building, resulting in the peaceful transition of power from President Shevardnadze to President Saakashvili.

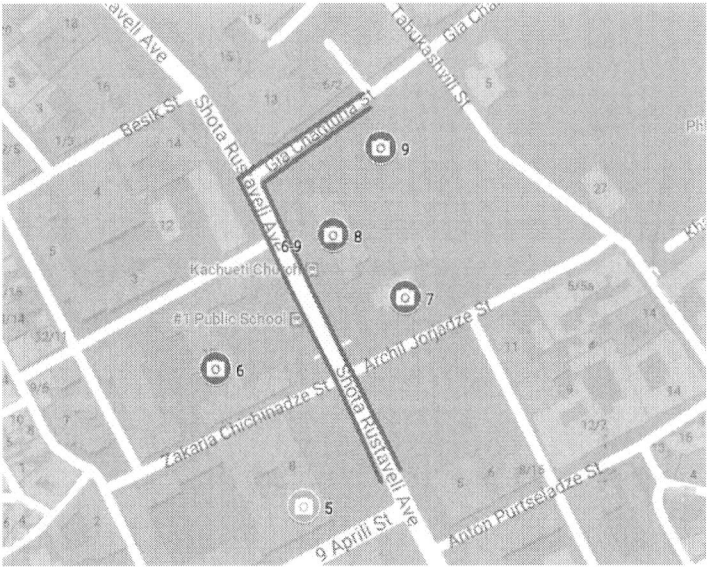

Map B: Georgian National Parliament to 9 April Park

Key:
  6. High School Number 1
  7. Kashveti Church of St. George
  8. Georgian National Gallery
  9. 9 April Park

High School Number 1

The next grand building a few more steps along Rustaveli Avenue is the former High School Number 1, or Classical Gymnasium *(Map B, Point 6)*. This beautiful U-shaped building, surrounding a courtyard planted with mature trees, is a faithful reproduction of the original 1802 structure that was burnt down during the 1991 Georgian Civil War. The

Russian government paid for this reconstruction, and the entire project took a remarkably short two years. During its time as a school, it educated many future leaders who would go on to play key roles in the development of Georgia.

Directly in front of the building are two statues on a single plinth. These are of Ilya Chavchavadze and Akaki Tsereteli, two nineteenth-century Georgian writers who espoused an independent and democratic country.

Chavchavadze is revered today as a national hero, and his fans refer to him as either 'The Uncrowned King' or 'Father of the Nation'. He regarded the three supporting columns of Georgian nationalism as territory, language and Christianity. His death at the hand of assassins galvanised independence movements, culminating in the declaration of independence in 1918.

Akaki Tsereteli, universally known throughout Georgia as just Akaki, was a prolific poet and national liberation movement leader. He published hundreds of patriotic poems, and together with his friend Chavchavadze, spearheaded the independence movement and tirelessly campaigned for a democratic Georgia free of Tsarist interference.

Kvashveti Church of Saint George

The Kvashveti Church *(Map B, Point 7)* was built quite recently around 1910 but stands on a site that has long held religious significance. In the sixth century, an Assyrian father, Davit Gareja, preached widely throughout Tbilisi and earned the wrath of fire-worshippers who resented his proselytising. According to legend, they bribed a pregnant woman to accuse him of adultery. Upon hearing this, Davit said that if this were indeed true she would give birth to a baby, and if not, a stone. The woman duly gave birth to a stone, and the name Kvashveti derives from this miracle, with 'Kva' meaning stone and 'shva' meaning give birth.

Soon after this occurrence, a church was erected. Hundreds of years later, in 1753, a new sturdier stone structure was built, which was eventually replaced by the church you see today. Its design takes as its inspiration the eleventh-century cathedral of Samtavisi, 60 km northwest of Tbilisi. Inside, the altar was painted by famous Tbilisi artist Ludo Gudiashvili, whose other works are in the Art Museum of Georgia.

Georgian National Gallery

The National Gallery *(Map B, Point 8)* can trace its roots back to the reign of Alexander III, who in the 1880s ordered the construction of a museum dedicated to Russian military history. The museum was intended to show the full glory of the Russian Empire in all of its colonies, something which understandably did not endear it to the locals. It was converted into the National Gallery in 1920 during the shortlived first Democratic Republic of Georgia. It had the broad aim of showcasing 'Georgian, and foreign work from all time periods and artistic movements'.

Today, you can see work from some of Georgia's great painters of the twentieth century, including Gudiashvili and Kakabadze. A highlight is the collection of thirty paintings by Pirosmanashvili who is considered to be one of the greatest artists of the past century, and whose work has been exhibited all around the world. His paintings include portraits of merchants, shopkeepers and workers, and also representations of animals and nature. They are primitivist in style, and do not concern themselves with getting into too much detail; figures often face directly out of the canvas and show little emotion, and some compositions are mainly monochrome. The gallery is open Tuesdays to Sundays from 10 am to 6 pm. The entrance fee is 7 GEL.

Once back on the pavement outside the gallery, look out for a bronze statue depicting a seated lady. The sculpture depicts Elene Akhvlediani, well known for her beautiful paintings of Georgian towns and villages, and for designing theatre sets for major productions in Tbilisi.

9 April Park

After a visit to the National Gallery, you can get a breath of fresh air and enjoy the green spaces of the nearby 9 April Park *(Map B, Point 9)*, which is directly behind the museum. This green space is one of the older parks of Tbilisi and is well known for its big, mature plane trees, which give welcome shade during sunny summer days. It is named to commemorate the sacrifices made by Georgian people during the 1989 anti-Soviet demonstrations.

There are many statues scattered throughout the park, including ones depicting painter Gudiashvili leaning nonchalantly on a lamppost, and Mihaly Zichy, a Hungarian artist well-liked in Georgia for his painting of Shota Rustaveli presenting his poem to Queen Tamar.

Now is a good time to escape the busy city streets and take a side trip up Mount Mtatsminda. To do so, you first need to walk uphill through a quiet and atmospheric neighbourhood of traditional Georgian houses in varying states of repair, and then take a ride to the peak on the Tbilisi Funicular.

From 9 April Park, walk back to Rustaveli Avenue and cross to the other side. Continue up the road for a short distance and turn left up Besik Street. Follow this up the steep hill. Where the street splits, take the left fork and continue up. It eventually becomes Mtatsminda Street. At the junction with Daniel Chonqadze Street, turn left, and the funicular station is on the right.

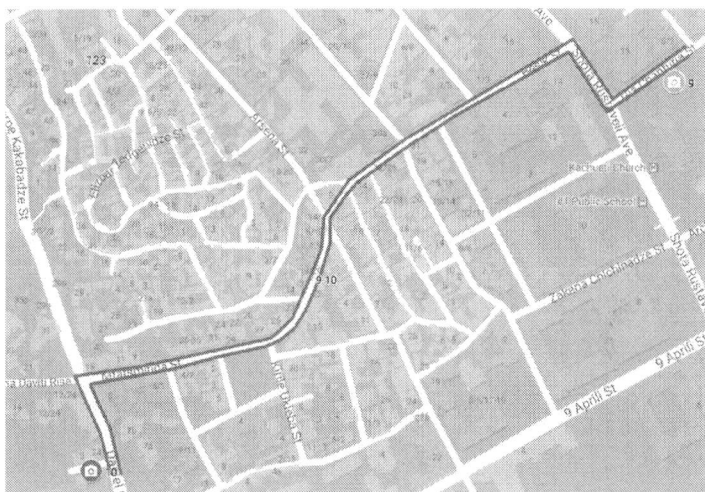

Map C: 9 April Park to Tbilisi Funicular and Mount Mtatsminda sights

Key:
10. Tbilisi Funicular

Tbilisi Funicular

The Tbilisi Funicular *(Map C, Point 10)* dates back all the way to 1905 and aimed to link the remote and undeveloped Mtatsminda plateau with the city 500 m below. When it first opened, the prospect of the cable pulling the carriage snapping terrified the residents to such an extent that they refused to get on board. The owner had to pay the passengers to use the funicular. Once people realised that it was perfectly safe, they queued up to buy tickets, and are still queuing today. So, this funicular has been transporting passengers up to the top of Mount Mtatsminda for well over a century. But don't worry, the operators comprehensively renovated the railway and carriages in 2012.

The lower cable car terminus on Chonqadze Street retains its original turn of the century architecture and resembles something between a fire station and a mosque. The funicular leaves every fifteen to twenty minutes. The cost is 2.5 GEL each way, and you pay with the Tbilisi public transport card; if you don't have one, you can buy one at the lower terminus. Once you leave the station, the journey takes around five minutes. There are spectacular views during the short trip.

The funicular is open daily from 9 am to 4 am.

Mount Mtatsminda

Once you emerge from the funicular carriage and the rather grand collonaded terminal, you are in Mtatsminda Park at the top of the mountain with the same name. The highest point in Tbilisi at a lofty 770 m, you get panoramic views of the entire city of Tbilisi, the surrounding countryside and on clear days the Caucasus mountains around Kazbegi. In the summer, it is also a bit cooler up here, and you can catch some refreshing breezes.

There are a few cafes and restaurants scattered around the area and an amusement park along with a 65 m high outsized Ferris wheel, a roller coaster and various other rides.

In recent years, the park has recently been subject to quite some controversy. It was acquired in the early 2000s by a Georgian billionaire named Badri Patarkatsishvili. However, in 2007, the government of Georgia led by then-president Saakashvili confiscated the businessman's assets, including the park, in response to his political activities which were deemed unwelcome. Patarkatsishvili died the year after, and it was only in 2012 when the government returned his assets to his widow. Saakashvili now faces criminal charges of illegal confiscation, along with many other pending legal actions as a result of his time in office.

Mtatsminda Parthenon and St. Davit's church

Mtstasminda Park also hosts the Georgian National Pantheon, halfway down the slopes of Mount Mtstasminda, in which the most prominent and influential contributors to Georgian culture are interred. These include those whose names you may have already encountered around Tbilisi: the writers and national liberation movement icons Ilia Chavchavadze and Akiko Tsereteli, the poets Giorgi Leonidze and Nikoloz Baratashvili, painter Lado Gudiashvili and theatre director Kote Marjanishvili. Curiously, the mother of Joseph Stalin is also buried here.

Next to the pantheon is the 'Mamadaviti' St. Davit's Church, built in the 1850s over the site of Davit Gareja's medieval cell and chapel. It is from here that the saint would leave his cell to preach the gospel in Tbilisi.

The easiest way to access these sites is to take the funicular down to the middle station. From here it is only a short walk along the hillside.

From the Pantheon, you have two options to get back to Shota Rustaveli Avenue. Firstly, walk down the narrow cobbled street, Mama Davita Rise, back down to its junction with Chonqadze Street. Keep going straight downhill along Mtatsminda street and then Besik Street until you reach the main avenue. Alternatively, retrace your steps back to the funicular station, where you can hop on the next carriage down. Once at the lower terminus, turn left and then take the first right down Mtatsminda Street, following the same route as above. Rustaveli Theatre will be facing you from across the street.

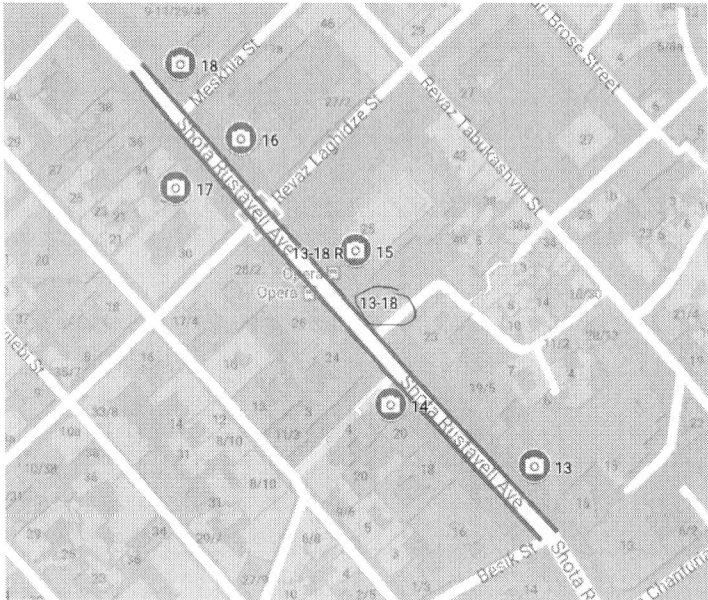

Map D: Rustaveli Theatre to Biltmore Hotel

Key:
  13. *Rustaveli Theatre*
  14. *Saxophone player sculpture*
  15. *Opera and Ballet Theatre*
  16. *Zurab Tsereteli Museum of Modern Art*
  17. *Prospero's Bookshop*
  18. *Biltmore Hotel*

* * *

Capitals of the Caucasus

Rustaveli Theatre

Rustaveli Theatre *(Map D, Point 13)* is one of the oldest and most prominent of Georgia's theatres, built in 1899 in a grand baroque rococo style. Inside, the theatre houses the main auditorium capable of seating more than eight hundred people, and two smaller stages. The famous Georgian painters Gudiashvili and Kakabadze, whose work we saw in the National Gallery, painted frescoes in the basement cafe. However, these were whitewashed over during the Soviet period, and are still undergoing restoration today.

For decades, the director of the theatre was the world-renowned Robert Sturua, famous throughout the art world for his Shakespeare productions. However, he was ignominiously sacked in 2011 after making xenophobic comments about the then-president, implying that a member of the Armenian ethnic minority should not hold such high office. Despite interventions by famous actors, he has not been reinstated.

The theatre's productions are mostly in Georgian, but they occasionally provide English subtitles. There is information on their latest playbill at www.rustavelitheatre.ge.

Saxophone player sculpture

As you walk up the left side of Shota Rustaveli Avenue and approach the junction with Miropan Laghidze Street, keep an eye out for a unique sculpture *(Map D, Point 14)* at number 22. It depicts a saxophone player emerging from the wall, with his torso, one knee and the tips of his shoes poking out from the masonry.

In addition to the saxophonist, many other modern

sculptures adorn the length of this avenue. Many of them depict old Georgian characters, sculpted by the young, self-taught Georgian artist Levan Bujiashvili. There were originally fifty installed, but due to some incidences of theft, forty-two remain. See how many you can spot during your walk!

Opera and Ballet Theatre

Another cultural hotspot of Tbilisi is just 100 m further up the avenue, and the dramatic pseudo-Moorish facade of the Opera and Ballet Theatre *(Map D, Point 15)* is one of the most distinctive in the city.

The theatre has had an unfortunate past and has kept the city's fire brigade busy. The original building opened in 1851 and was one of the many cultural projects undertaken by Governor Vorontsov, yet unfortunately burnt down to the ground in 1874. It was replaced in the 1890s by the magnificent Moorish structure designed by P. Sretter. However, this also burned down in the 1970s, leaving only the front facade, foyer and some side walls. Luckily for us, it was comprehensively reconstructed to preserve its original appearance.

The theatre now stages a packed schedule of opera and ballet throughout the year, and its troupes embark upon extensive international tours. The internationally-successful Georgian tenor Badri Maysuradze currently leads acts as Artistic Director of the theatre, while decorated prima ballerina Nina Ananiashvili heads the ballet troupe. Full programme information, in English, is available on their website at www.opera.ge.

* * *

Zurab Tsereteli Museum of Modern Art (MOMA)

One block further up Rustaveli Avenue on the same side of the street as the Opera and Ballet Theatre is the Museum of Modern Art *(Map D, Point 16)*. It displays many examples of modern Georgian art, almost entirely from Zurab Tsereteli, the Georgian-born painter and sculptor after whom the museum takes its name. He founded MOMA in Tbilisi and made a grant of two thousand works from his private collection.

Tsereteli is the president of the Russian Academy of Arts and acts as a kind of patriarch of the national art scene. He's a fascinating character, little known in the west, but is probably the most commercially successful living artist in Russia. His work rate is prodigious, to say the least, with hundreds of paintings and dozens of over-sized public sculptures standing throughout Russia and around the world.

MOMA Tbilisi spreads over three floors of beautifully lit and spacious galleries. One level exhibits his large, colourful paintings, another his sketches and the last shows artefacts and displays detailing his long life. You can also see some of his sculptures scattered throughout the building.

The museum is open Tuesdays to Sundays from 11 am to 6 pm, and the entrance fee is 5 GEL.

Prospero's Bookshop

Opposite MOMA is a wonderful English language bookshop *(Map D, Point 17)*. Cross the road, and walk through the archway into the hidden internal courtyard. The bookshop has a great selection of titles you would not easily find back home, including translated Georgian fiction, other south

Caucasus novels and a nice range of local travel literature. Maps are also available. This shop is a real find for all bookworms.

You can relax then relax in the courtyard flicking through your new purchases while sipping a coffee from the neighbouring Caliban Coffee Shop.

Prospero's is open daily from 9.30 am to 8 pm.

Biltmore Hotel

Look across the street, and to the left of the MOMA, you will see the Stalinist collonaded facade of a building which was constructed in 1938 to house the Institute of Marxism-Leninism. Its use now couldn't be more different and is safe to say that the two revolutionary leaders will be spinning in their graves. Today, it is the home of the recently-opened five-star Biltmore Hotel *(Map D, Point 18)*, the first to be built outside the United States. The new skyscraper behind this older building, which to some literally sticks out like a sore thumb, was constructed as part of the hotel complex.

The Stalinist structure was originally slated to be almost entirely demolished, leaving behind just one facade. However, a public outcry and protests by preservationists eventually prevented this cultural vandalism from happening.

Continue following Rustaveli Avenue as it curves to the left around the outer fringes of Rose Revolution Square. The next grand building on your left will be the Georgian National Academy of Sciences.

* * *

Capitals of the Caucasus

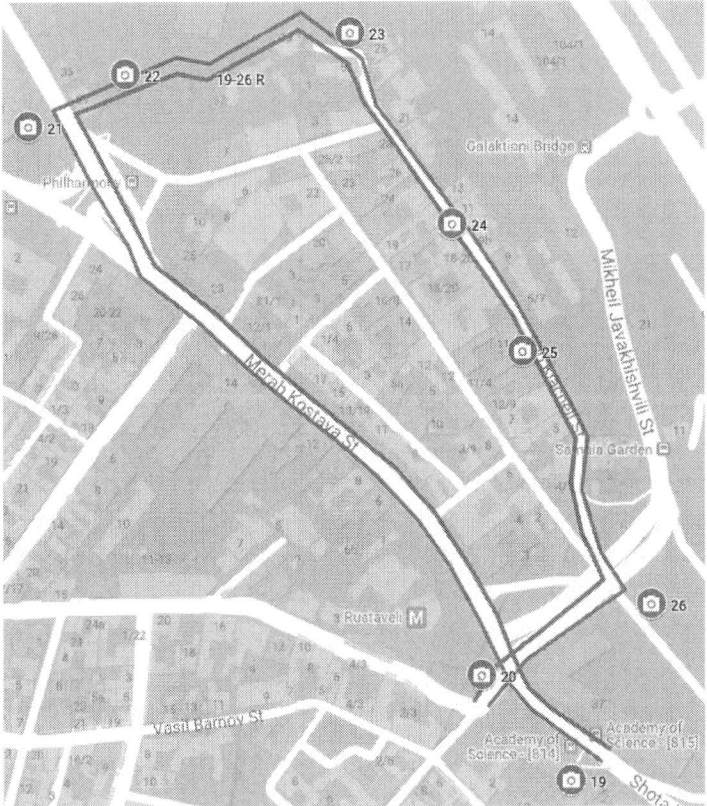

Map E: Georgian National Academy of Sciences to Rose
Revolution Square

Key:
  19. *Georgian National Academy of Sciences*
  20. *Rustaveli Square*
  21. *Tbilisi Concert Hall*
  22. *Vera Park*
  23. *Lurji Monastery*
  24. *Vera Pub Streets*
  25. *Elena Akhvledianai Museum*

Georgian National Academy of Sciences

The Georgian National Academy of Sciences *(Map E, Point 19)* was established in 1941 and continues to be the principle learned society of the country. It coordinates scientific research, supervises forty scientific institutes and promotes international collaborations.

The building is another example of classic socialist architecture, built in the 1950s following an architectural competition. The long front of the building faces Rustaveli Avenue while its shorter western section looks out onto Rustaveli Square, and where the two facades meet there is a 55 m tower topped with a metal steeple. Usually, at most times of the day, there are dozens of souvenir sellers in front of the building, with their wares arranged on the steps. It's a good place to pick up a bargain, after a bit of negotiating of course.

Rustaveli Square

Cross Kakabadzeebi Street from the Academy of Sciences and you'll be in the small Rustaveli Square *(Map E, Point 20)*. Here you can find the red line Rustaveli metro station and on a corner the prominent McDonalds restaurant, which was the very first to be opened in Georgia.

Pride of place in the centre of the square is a statue of the great poet Shota Rustaveli himself. He stands on a tall rectangular plinth, at the base of which are reliefs showing scenes from his masterpiece 'The Knight in the Panther's

Skin'. This is where the Rustaveli Avenue comes to an end.

Beyond the square, Rustaveli Avenue becomes Kostava Street and enters the trendy Vera district.

Continue to walk straight, along Kostava Street.

Tbilisi Concert Hall

This modern round building *(Map E, Point 21)* plays host to Georgian and international artists and bands. Here the road splits, with Kostava Street passing to the right of the hall. Look to the right, and you will see the entrance to Vera Park.

Vera Park

Vera Park *(Map E, Point 22)* is a beautiful green space at the heart of the Vera district, filled with pine trees and winding pathways. It's a relaxing place to enjoy a snack or drink from one of the stall vendors.

The 1970s late Soviet Modernist building in the centre of the park is the Chess Club, named after the five-time world chess champion, Georgian-born Nona Gaprindashvili. The whole building is planned around a 500-plus seat auditorium which hosts high profile chess games.

Walk to the right of the chess palace to the edge of the park, and you should find some steps leading down to two churches.

Lurji Monastery

'Lurji' in Georgian translates as blue, and this name derives from the glazed blue tiled roof of the church. Dedicated to St. Andrew, it dates from the end of the twelfth century. It has been damaged and renovated many times over, so what you see today is a mix of construction from different periods *(Map E, Point 23)*. Only the lower half of the southern wall, the eastern facade and a few rows of stones within the northern and western walls remain. Extravagant frescoes decorate just about every square inch of the interior.

In the mid-nineteenth century, during Russian rule, the conical Georgian-style dome was replaced with a Russian Orthodox-style onion dome, creating an uneasy hybrid. The offending dome was only restored after independence in 1990. In Soviet times, further indignities were heaped on the church, and it was first used as a sawmill and then as a museum of medicine.

Next to Lurji Monastery is the bigger, onion-domed Russian Orthodox church dedicated to St. John the Theologian. The church was built at the turn of the twentieth century under the orders of then-Governor Golicin. Compared with its more richly decorated neighbour, the interior is mostly simple white and light blue plasterwork. The most colourful spot in the entire church is the golden iconostasis in front of the altar.

Vera 'Pub Streets'

Beginning from just outside Lurji Monastery is Kiacheli Street *(Map E, Point 24)*. Together with its parallel sister Akhvledian (or Petrovskaya) Street, these two narrow streets are lined with pubs and restaurants and are one of the liveliest areas for nightlife in the whole of Tbilisi. It's a great place to come back to in the evening.

From the monastery, remain on Kiacheli Street. Down towards the bottom of the street is the Elena Akhvlediani Museum, on the right-hand side.

Elena Akhvlediani Museum

Elena Akhvlediani, one of the most prominent Georgian artists of the twentieth century, lived much of her life at 12 Kiacheli Street *(Map E, Point 24)*. As you may remember, there is also a statue to Elena Akhvlediani outside the National Gallery. When she died in 1975, she bequeathed her home to the Georgian National Museum so that the public could experience for themselves where she lived and work.

During her time in the house, Akhvlediani hosted many gatherings for Georgia's leading artists and often staged exhibition evenings showing her latest work. The house has a unique and compelling atmosphere built up over the years of her artistic endeavours, and this is still very much evident today. It has a typical Georgian interior, and there are more than three thousand artefacts including paintings, theatrical sketches, illustrations, photos and personal items.

As well as painting life in Georgian towns and villages, Akhvlediani also designed sets for the Marjanishvili Theatre and illustrated the works of national hero and liberation movement leader Ilia Chavchavadze.

Rose Revolution Square

By strolling down to the end of Kiacheli Street, you will emerge into the wide, open expanse of the Rose Revolution Square *(Map E, Point 26)*. This wide open space was built in 1983 and called Republic Square. Its name was later changed to commemorate the 2003 uprising which resulted in the peaceful transition of power.

Protests started when international observers declared that the elections held at the beginning of November 2003 fell short of international standards. The demonstrations lasted for three weeks and reached their peak on 22 November when opposition party supporters burst into the parliament, clutching roses, and forced the then-president Eduard Shevardnadze to flee. Soon after he called for the support of the military, but they refused, prompting him to resign. New presidential and parliamentary elections saw the old Soviet leader replaced by Mikheil Saakashvili.

A short walk to the west of Rose Revolution Square brings you back to Rustaveli Square, where this walking tour ends.

At the Rustaveli Square metro station, you can catch a red line train back to Freedom Square, or if you feel energetic stroll back along Rustaveli Avenue.

Tbilisi Walking Tour 2 - Wandering west of the Mtkvari River

Gorgasali Square

Gorgasali Square *(Map F, Point 27)* is the starting point for this walking tour of the neighbourhoods roughly to the west and southwest of the Mtkvari river.

Today, the square is a bustling crossroads, often with queues of traffic honking their horns. Things were not that much different back in the seventeenth and eighteenth centuries when the square was the site of a crowded bazaar attracting traders from Russia, the Middle East and from along the Silk Road. Instead of traffic jams, camel trains would have brought spices, carpets and silk, while Georgians would have sold weapons, wine, metalwork and woollen goods.

From the square, Vakhtang Gorgasali Street heads off south down the river towards Abanotubani (see walking tour 3), and the Metekhi bridge crosses the Mtkvari river to the east bank (see walking tour 4).

This tour will instead go north, plunging deep into the winding alleyways of the old town, starting with Shardeni

Street.

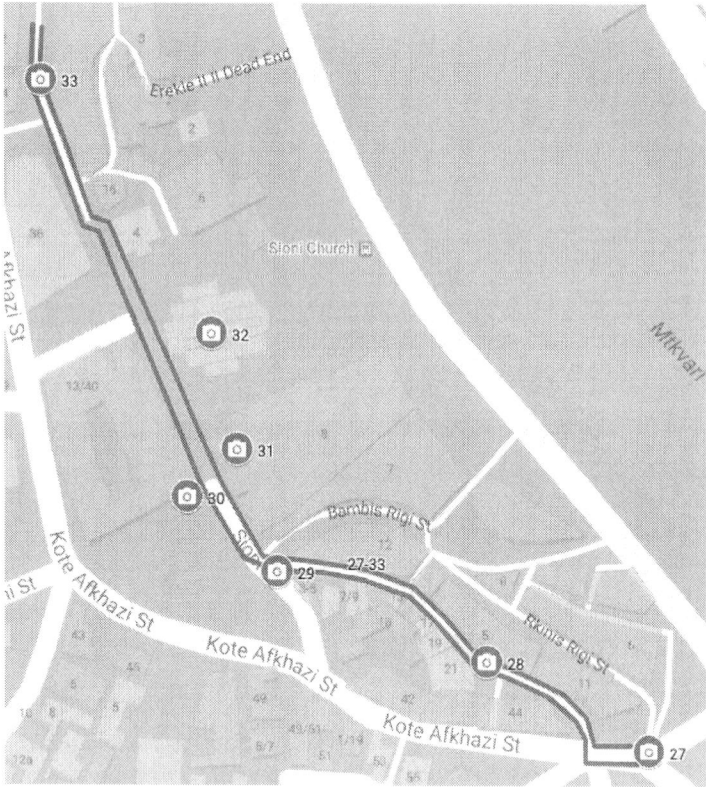

Map F: Gorgasali Square to Erekle II Street

Key:
27. *Gorgasali Square*
28. *Shardeni Street*
29. *Toastmaster Statue*
30. *Hidden bakery*
31. *Tbilisi History Museum*
32. *Sioni Cathedral*
33. *Erekle II Street*

Capitals of the Caucasus

* * *

Shardeni Street

Walk out of the square, away from the river, along Kote Afkhazi Street and take Shardeni Street *(Map F, Point 28)* on the immediate right. This picturesque narrow thoroughfare takes its name from Jan Chardin, the French explorer who visited Tbilisi in the mid-nineteenth century.

You can have a relaxing walk along this pedestrianised street while admiring the grapevine-covered houses. This street is a magnet for tourists, and here you can find every imaginable restaurant and souvenir shop.

Toastmaster statue

Where Shardeni Street meets Sioni Street, you can see the statue of the toastmaster *(Map F, Point 29)*, perched somewhat precariously in the middle of the junction. This sculpture shows a tamada, someone who plays an essential role in Georgian feasts, weddings and other special occasions.

The statue depicts a man about to take a sip from a cow's horn drinking vessel and is modelled on a much earlier figurine from the ancient kingdom of Colchis on the Black Sea coast of modern-day Georgia. Incidentally, Colchis was famous in Greek mythology as the destination of the Argonauts and the home of the Golden Fleece. In Colchian times, the Pagan population worshipped various idols, and foremost among these was the moon, with people often sacrificing bulls in its honour. Bull horns are crescent-shaped and reminiscent of the phase of the moon associated with new life and rejuvenation, and were accordingly used by tamadas at feasts for toasts.

Tamadas were crucial to the success of a gathering and celebrants chose them with extreme care. Above all, they needed to be eloquent, and indeed some of the best tamadas were accomplished poets and writers. They also needed to organise entertainment well, be aware of sensitivities and politics among the guests, and control the pace of toasting according to the level of inebriation!

Even today you can see horns make an appearance at weddings, and all self-respecting gift shops in Tbilisi have a few for sale among all the other souvenirs.

'Hidden' bakery

From the Toastmaster statue, turn right up Sioni Street. If you are feeling peckish and in the mood for a quick snack, then pay close attention to the building ahead on the left *(Map F, Point 30)*. At its corner, you will see a set of doors from which a staircase descends. Down there in a vaulted basement, you will find a busy bakery, churning out a vast selection of hot Georgian bread and pastries straight from the oven. You shouldn't miss out on this culinary treat, but if you have difficulty finding it ask a local and they will know how to get there for sure.

Tbilisi History Museum

Continuing up Sioni Street, and you'll find the Tbilisi History Museum *(Map F, Point 31)* after a few short steps. This institution is in a restored three-storey caravanserai, which used to provide accommodation to weary travellers on the old Silk Road.

The museum's permanent exhibition displays artefacts from prehistory up to the present day, with an emphasis on the last two centuries. On the ground floor, several shops offer for sale local art, pottery and jewellery.

The museum is open daily from 10 am to 6 pm, except Mondays.

Sioni Cathedral of the Dormition

The compact Sioni Cathedral *(Map F, Point 32)*, right next to the Tbilisi History Museum, is one of the landmarks of Tbilisi's old quarter. It takes its name from the Zion hill in Jerusalem which is the location of the city of David.

King Vakhtang Gorgasali ordered the construction of the church way back in the fifth century, yet building work only began one hundred years later in 575. They completed its construction in the early seventh century. However, the structure you see today is not the medieval original, thanks to the particularly turbulent and violent Georgian history, and the first church was destroyed by invading Arabs. King David IV, one of the greatest and most successful rulers of Georgia, rebuilt the church, and the fundamental parts of today's structure date from then. Subsequent conquests by Timur, and later the Persians, saw extensive restorations in the fifteenth and seventeenth centuries, and a major earthquake in 1668 prompted further renovations.

The church is made from a yellowish volcanic rock called tuff, quarried from an area to the southwest of Tbilisi, and is an archetypal example of medieval Georgian church architecture. The cross-shaped plan of the structure is much squarer than churches in western Europe. At the centre of the cross is a tall drum topped with a conical dome. You'll see this church design throughout Tbilisi and at some of the famous hilltop sites such as Gergeti.

While the exterior of Sioni Cathedral is mostly without any ornamentation, dazzling frescoes cover the inside. Those in the dome and upper parts of the cathedral date from the 1840-50s and were painted by the Russian nobleman and military administrator, Prince Grigory Gagarin. The lower frescoes are quite modern, painted in 1989 by Georgian artist Levan Tsutskiridze.

The highlight of the cathedral and the reason for its unique significance for Georgians is the grapevine cross of Saint Nino, a major symbol of the Georgian Orthodox Church. Saint Nino purportedly received this directly from the Virgin Mary, and then secured it by entwining her hair. She introduced Christianity to Georgia and carried the cross, which is particularly distinctive due to its drooping arms, on her evangelical mission. Throughout its long history, it has been hidden at many locations to protect it from invading armies, and it has resided at the Sioni Cathedral since 1802. The one you see is a replica; the original is kept safe somewhere deep within the cathedral. Also inside are the tombs of many Catholicos-Patriarchs, the heads of the Georgian Orthodox Church.

Outside again, to the north of the cathedral, you'll see a freestanding three-storey belfry. King Alexander the First built this bell tower during one of the main reconstructions, this time repairing the damage wrought by invading Timurid forces. Don't confuse this with another three-storey bell tower across the street; that one was built in 1812 to commemorate Russian victory over the Ottoman empire.

Erekle II Street

Continuing north from Sioni Cathedral, Sioni Street becomes Erekle II Street *(Map F, Point 33)* after a few metres. This street, entirely lined with bars and restaurants, is named after Heraclius II. This king, also known as Erekle II, reigned over the Georgian regions of Kartli and Kakheti in the latter half of the eighteenth centuries.

The rows of bars and cafes come to an end at the junction of Antimoz Ivereli Lane. Turn right here for a brief detour to see the Bridge of Peace.

* * *

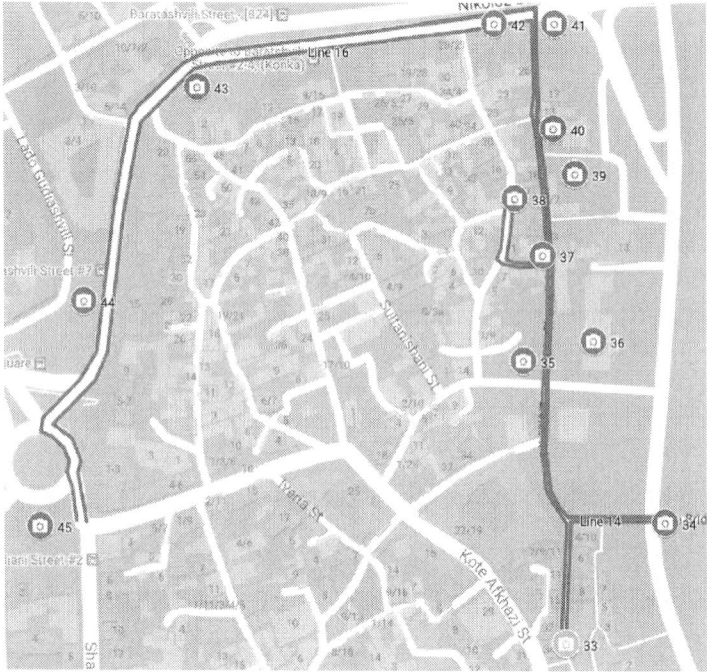

Map G: Erekle II Street to Tbilisi Town Hall

Key:

34. *Bridge of Peace*
35. *Erekles Square*
36. *Patriarchate of Georgia*
37. *Kari St George Church*
38. *Nikoloz Baratashvili Museum*
39. *Anchiskhati Basilica*
40. *Rezo Gabriadze Puppet Theatre*
41. *Berikaoba Statue*
42. *Baratashvili Street*
43. *Ancient City Walls*
44. *Pushkin Park*
45. *Tbilisi Town Hall*

Bridge of Peace

This striking 150-metre long pedestrian bridge *(Map G, Point 34)* spanning the Mtkvari river is a relatively new addition to the Tbilisi cityscape, completed in 2010. It was commissioned to connect the old town on the west bank with the new quarters over on the east. The architects built the entire bridge in Italy in various modules, transported them across Europe in two hundred trucks and then assembled the structure on site.

The bridge is unreservedly modernist, constructed from steel with a curving glass canopy. At night, the thousands of embedded LED lights within its structure come to life, producing a shimmering light display. It communicates, in Morse code, the chemical elements found in the human body. The intention is to celebrate life and peace between people by telling the story of what makes up each one of us.

Such an incongruous feature placed next to the old town has attracted its fair share of criticism, although it seems to be a firm favourite with visitors and a popular selfie spot. As you walk to the centre of the bridge, you can enjoy panoramic views of pretty much all the significant landmarks of Tbilisi, including Metekhi Church, the Vakhtang Gorgasali statue, Narikala fortress, Rike Park and the Presidential Palace.

Retrace your steps back along the bridge to where you began, then turn right to continue along Erekles II Street.

Erekles Square

Further ahead you come to Erekles Square *(Map G, Point 35)*, a leafy park with cobbled walkways which until the mid-nineteenth century was the famous central square of the whole of Tbilisi. It was also known as Batoni's (Lord's) Square because the palace of King Rustam stood on this spot until invading Persian forces ruined it in 1795.

On the northern edge of the square, you will see the ornate balconies of the palace of King Giorgi XII, the last king of Georgia. His reign was shortlived, beginning in 1798 and ending with his death in 1800, at which point Georgia became part of the Russian Empire.

From Erekles Square, Erekle II Street becomes the narrow Ione Shavteli Street, the commercial heart of the old city in medieval times.

Patriarchate of Georgia

Across the street from Erekles Square is the imposing bulk of the Patriarchate of Georgia *(Map G, Point 36)*, built on the site of the destroyed palace of King Rustam. Initially intended as a governor's residence and administrative block, religious authorities procured the building in 1848, and it has had an ecclesiastical use ever since. Today it houses the headquarters of the Georgian Orthodox Church.

This religion plays a dominant role in Georgian life, counting more than 84% of the population as followers. It has been the state religion for pretty much all of the sixteen or so centuries since its introduction by Saint Nino, except during the Soviet years, and is considered to be the country's most influential institution. It is currently headed by Catholicos-Patriarch Ilia II, who has held the position for more than forty years.

* * *

Kari Saint George Church

Just to the northern of Erekles Square is the diminutive Kari church *(Map G, Point 37)*. A much older church built by Vakhtang Gorgasali (who also ordered the construction of Sioni Cathedral) originally stood on this site. With much else, it was destroyed by the Mongols in their late fourteenth-century rampage through the city. Eventually, in the 1640s, three new churches were built here using the rubble from the original structure, dedicated to Saint John, the Annunciation, and Saint George, with only the last surviving today. For much of its life the church has operated as the court church, hence its name 'Kari'.

Nikoloz Baratashvili Memorial House

Walk down the small alleyway running past the church, away from Shavteli Street, and then right onto Chakhrukhadze Street. Number seventeen on the right-hand side is the house in which the Georgian romantic poet Nikoloz Baratashvili lived, now a memorial museum *(Map G, Point 38)*. In this part of town, you will also see a major road and bridge named after him and on the other bank of the river a prominent statue.

Baratashvili is a giant of Georgian literature, and spearheaded the development of nineteenth-century Georgian literature and introducing 'Europeanism'. He died when he was only twenty-six, and so his works only comprise forty short lyrics, a longer poem and some private letters. Nonetheless, fans sometimes refer to him as Georgia's Byron.

The museum displays many different artefacts related to

the great poet's life, including furniture, folk musical instruments, paintings, manuscripts and books. As 2017 marked the two hundredth anniversary of his birth, the Tbilisi museum authority undertook a comprehensive renovation and introduced 3D animation holograms and multimedia displays to tell the story of Baratashvili.

Anchiskhati Basilica

Retrace your steps back down Chakhrukhadze Street, turn left and then left again and you'll find yourself back on Shatvali Street. After a few short steps, you will come across one of the old town's highlights, and longest surviving church, the sixth-century Anchiskhati Basilica *(Map G, Point 39)*. It was purportedly built by King Dachi of Iberia when he made Tbilisi his capital.

The church was originally dedicated to the Virgin Mary. However, its name was changed in 1675 when the precious twelfth-century icon of the Saviour was moved there from the remote Ancha monastery to prevent it falling into the hands of Ottoman marauders (Anchiskhati means 'icon of Ancha).

As with many churches and important buildings in Tbilisi, the basilica has been through the wars a bit and accordingly has had a few renovations and reconstructions. In the seventeenth century, some parts of the upper church and the bell tower were rebuilt in brick, and in the 1870s a dome was added. The oldest and most original parts of the church are the walls, constructed from the same yellow tuff material used in for the Sioni Cathedral.

The interior is dark and mysterious, lightened somewhat by the many devotional candles. Most of the paintings date from the nineteenth century, except for those in the altar screen which were commissioned by the then Catholicos-

Patriarch of Georgia, Nikoloz Amilakhvari.

The church was closed down during the Soviet era and converted to a museum of handicrafts. However, following independence, it resumed its central role in the religious life of Georgia. It is home to the Anchiskhati choir, which is known throughout choral circles globally as one of the best performers of Georgian polyphonic choral music.

Around the embankment side of the church, you will see a sculpture showing the head of Nodar Dumbadze, one of the most popular Georgian writers of the last century. Most of his novels have since been made into films. His early books, such as Granny, Iliko, Illarion and I (1960) and I See the Sun (1962) are semi-autobiographical and gives a fascinating insight into Georgian village life during World War Two.

Rezo Gabriadze Puppet Theatre and Clock Tower

Back on Shatvali Street, continue north, and you will come across an apparently ancient and slightly ramshackle clock tower (Map G, Point 40), which looks as if it has been plucked directly from the pages of a fairy tale. However, don't let appearances deceive you. The tower was erected only in 2010 by the renowned Georgian artist, writer and director Rezo Gabriadze. He designed the tower himself, using a mix of medieval architectural features so that it blends harmoniously with the surrounding old town. At the top of every hour, an angel comes out of the tower to ring the bell with her hammer, so if you are walking past at this time make sure you stop to watch.

The puppet theatre itself, while modest in size, is well-regarded internationally as a preeminent cultural institution, with high-quality marionette performances. The theatre also makes extensive tours and has brought its show to New York,

London, Edinburgh, Toronto and Moscow among other far-flung venues.

The original and particularly moving plays comprising the repertoire of the theatre were all written by Gabriadze, and include *Stalingrad*, a requiem for the great battle, and *The Autumn of My Spring* which tells the story of life in impoverished post-war Georgia.

Gabriadze is also famous for the films that he has written, including *Don't Grieve*, *Mimino* and *Kin-Dza-Dza*. His characters from Mimino are immortalised in the sculpture nearby the Avlabari metro station on the other side of the Mtkvari river.

You should book in advance as performances tend to fill up quickly.

Berikaoba sculpture

At the end of Shatveli Street, on the corner at the junction with Baratashvili is the Berikaoba sculpture *(Map G, Point 41)*, showing an old Pagan festival where actors parade childishly and playfully through village streets.

The principal characters are a bride and a groom, accompanied by several men (berika) disguised as common Georgian animals such as the wolf, bear and boar. Their wedding is broken up by marauding Tatars, who proceed to kill the groom and kidnap the bride. The berika eventually resuscitate the groom with healing water and minerals, who then goes on to chase the Tatars and rescue the bride. The performance ends with a lavish Georgian feast, the supra.

The festival is held around the time of the spring equinox and celebrates the rebirth of nature. It aims to ensure a fertile and fruitful agricultural year ahead.

The sculpture exudes joy and cheerfulness and brings out

the playful nature of the Berikaoba festival. Passers-by are free to enter the circle and pose with the statues any way they see fit and is a great photo opportunity!

Baratashvili Street

Walking from the Berikaoba statue, away from the river along Baratashvili Street *(Map G, Point 42)*, you will start to see remains of the old Tbilisi walls. The division between the older and newer parts of the city is apparent here. On the right-hand side of the street are the relatively modern blocks constructed in the 1950s and 1960s. The street plan extending outwards from that side is more regular and grid-like. On the left side, there are the old eighteenth-century city walls topped by handsome balconied buildings. Many of these now function as restaurants. These walls were uncovered in the 1970s when existing buildings were demolished when Georgian architect Shota Kavlashvili redeveloped this part of the city. There is a statue to this architect at the end of this stretch of wall.

Ancient city walls

Further along, Baratashvili Street becomes Pushkin Street. At this point, the remains of twelfth and thirteenth-century walls *(Map G, Point 43)* were discovered when Pushkin Street was renovated in 2012. Many fragments of twelfth-century glazed pottery were also found. The municipality built bridges to protect all this archaeology, and today the road and pavements pass safely overhead. Pedestrian walkways were also made under the bridges so that visitors can view the walls up close.

The remains included several towers, and you can see multiple layers showing that they had repeatedly been destroyed by invaders and then subsequently rebuilt with different materials. The last destruction of the walls was in 1801 when the Russian Empire annexed Georgia. Roads and buildings were built on top of the ruins in the intervening years, and the walls were forgotten until their recent unearthing.

Pushkin Park

Pushkin Street, named after the famous Russian poet and author, eventually leads you to Pushkin Park *(Map G, Point 44)* on the left, also named after the great man. This pretty little green space is an extension of Freedom Square.

As well as a statue of Pushkin, the park also contains the grave of Kamo, a Bolshevik revolutionary and early confidante of Stalin, whose real name was Simon Petrosian. Kamo carried out many militant operations in Georgia in the first few years of the twentieth century. The most dramatic of these was the robbing of vast sums of money from a bank in Freedom Square. Kamo personally delivered the cash to Lenin to help fund further revolutionary activities. He came to a sticky end in 1922 when he was run over by a truck while cycling in Tbilisi, widely believed to have been the work of assassins under Stalin's orders. It is ironic that his grave is in full view of the bank that he robbed years earlier. The monument has since been removed, but the grave itself, now unmarked, is somewhere between the fountain and Pushkin's statue.

* * *

Tbilisi Town Hall

Across Freedom Square is the Tbilisi Town Hall *(Map G, Point 45)*, with its impressive facade and clock tower topped by the fluttering Georgian flag. This building contains the mayor's office and the City Assembly. Most of the departments managing the city, such as transport, educations, welfare and urban planning, are housed within its walls.

The town hall was built during Russian rule in the 1830s but has since experienced many renovations and reconstructions. The present facade is the result of an ambitious redesign by architect Paul Stern in the neo-Moorish style that was all the rage at that time. The clock tower is even more modern, added in 1912.

As you face the Town Hall, walk down Kote Afghazi street leaving Freedom Square on your left. Continue straight then turn right down Abesadze Street. Then after 200 m or so turn left onto Anton Katalikos Street.

* * *

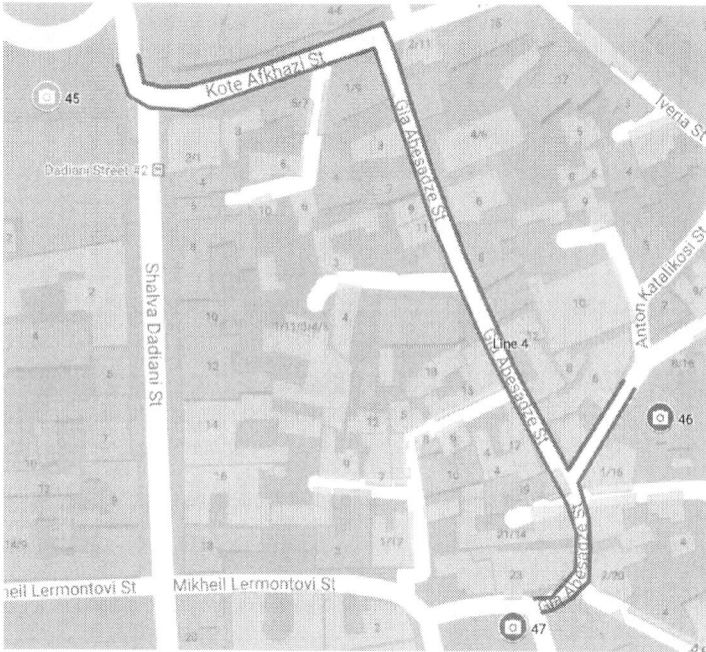

Map H: Tbilisi Town Hall to Lado Gudiashvili Square

Key:
   45. Tbilisi Town Hall
   46. David Baazov Museum of the History of the Jews
   47. Lado Gudiashvili Square

David Baazov Museum of the History of the Jews

The David Baazov Museum *(Map H, Point 46)* is at 3 Anton Katalikos Street, housed in a distinctive, red-brick, dome-shaped former synagogue. It was established in 1933 to tell the centuries-long history of Jewish life in Georgia, and to study Jewish-Georgian relations. This quite small but never fascinating museum displays interesting artefacts such as Torahs, menorah candelabra, religious clothing, paintings, photographs and other documents.

The Jewish community in Georgia is one of the oldest in the country, with the first migration occurring in the sixth century BC following the Babylonian siege of Jerusalem. Since then, up until Soviet times, the Jews and other Georgians lived harmoniously with an almost total lack of anti-Semitism. The USSR, however, terminated Zionist activity in the country, and the Jewish community's situation only improved in the 1990s when Georgia obtained its independence.

David Baazov was a Georgian-born Jew who became a prominent rabbi at the turn of the century. He organised an all-Jewish Congress in Tbilisi at the end of World War I, which brought together delegations from every Jewish community in the country. He also established Jewish schools across Georgia, founded a Jewish newspaper and organised migration to Israel following a Soviet crackdown on Jewish institutions. In Stalin's 1938 purge, he was arrested and exiled to Siberia. He returned to Georgia in 1945 but died soon after that.

The museum is open daily from 11 am to 5 pm.

From the museum, retrace your steps along Anton Katalikos Street and then turn left onto Abesadze Street. Continue until you reach Lado Gudiashvili Square.

Lado Gudiashvili Square

The quaint, cobbled Lado Gudiashvili Square *(Map H, Point 47)*, is named after the twentieth-century painter and famous son of Tbilisi. His paintings had strong mythological and poetic themes and are seen to combine the traditions of Georgian art with that of French symbolism. Some of Gudiashvili's works hang in the Art Museum of Georgia.

Crumbling nineteenth and early twentieth century buildings, replete with distinctive wrought-iron balconies surround the square on all sides. These are original facades, and minimal restoration has been done over the past century, giving the area an unforgettable atmosphere.

However, recent urban development policies have thrust the area into controversy. In 2011, the plans of an Austrian consortium prompted the establishment by residents of an 'Occupy Gudiashvili' movement to stop what they saw as cultural vandalism. The action generated considerable media coverage, and the plans were eventually shelved. At the time of writing, in 2018, the mayor has officially kicked off a more sympathetic renovation project which aims to fully restore eighteen prominent buildings and preserve the area's cultural heritage.

Walk down the western edge of the square and exit on Beglar Akhospireli Street. After 100 m you will reach Asatiani Street. Cross the street and continue straight along Betlemi Rise.

* * *

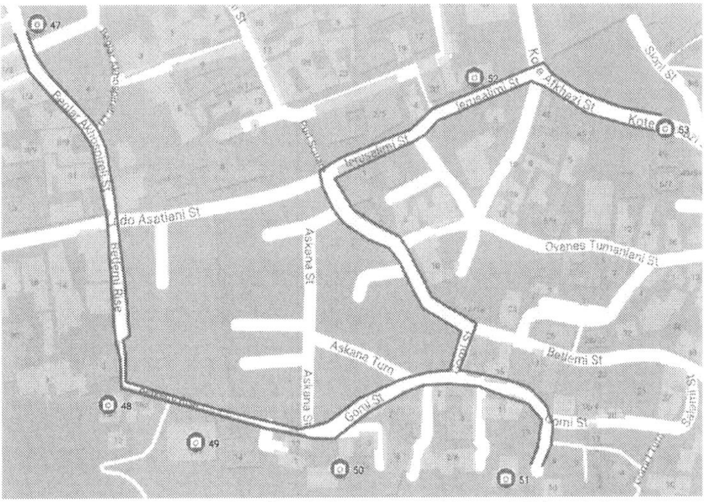

Map I: Lado Gudiashvili Square to Kote Afkhazi Street

Key:
  47. *Lado Gudiashvili Square*
  48. *Lower Betlemi Church*
  49. *Upper Betlemi Church*
  50. *Ateshgah Fire Temple*
  51. *Kldisubani St. Geroge Church*
  52. *Jvaris Mama and Noroshen Churches*
  53. *Kotc Afkhazi Street*

Betlemi Neighbourhood

This district is one of the oldest in the whole of Tbilisi and nestles against the slopes which lead up to the Narikala fortress. It traces its history back to the very founding of Tbilisi, and the winding layout of the streets is evidence of this neighbourhood's long past. Most of the houses you see are built over the remains, or incorporate parts, from much older predecessors.

This area is built on a series of terraces connected by narrow lanes and street stairs. Its a maze of balconied old houses, churches and courtyards. Yes, it is damaged, faded and non-maintained, but this only adds to its beauty and atmosphere.

Lower Betlemi Church

The first church you encounter on the right is Lower Betlemi *(Map I, Point 48)*. This site originally had a nunnery and a small chapel, built by Armenians emigrating from Iran in the early eighteenth century. The current structure was built in 1868 and continued to be used as an Armenian place of worship right up until 1988 when it was handed over to the Georgian Orthodox Church. In the intervening years, it has been 'Georganised', with the removal of specific inscriptions and architectural features, and the addition of new Georgian frescoes.

Upper Betlemi Church

A few more steps along Betlemi Rise you come across Upper Betlemi Church *(Map I, Point 49)*. Legend has it that the original church on this site was built by King Vakhtang Gorgali way back in the sixth century. Whatever the veracity of this very early history, we know that the Armenians established the Virgin Mary Church here in the fifteenth century, which was replaced by the construction of the current church in 1740.

* * *

Capitals of the Caucasus

Ateshgah Fire Temple

Continue walking along Betlemi Rise to its junction with Gomi Street, where you will find the remains of a fifth-century Zoroastrian fire temple *(Map I, Point 50)*. To get up close to the Ateshgah is rather tricky, and you will need to weave through the courtyards of the neighbourhood to get there.

Ateshgah resembles an old cube made from red brick. It is thought to have been built during the time of the Persian Sasanid empire, and the name 'Ateshgah' means 'the place for fire' in Persian. It is one of the very oldest structures in Tbilisi.

Zoroastrianism has the distinction of being the world's first monotheistic religion and takes its name from its founder, the Persian prophet Zoroaster. Adherents to the faith worshipped a god called Ahura Mazda, and fire was the most important symbol of the religion as it was considered to represent his holy spirit. For centuries Zoroastrianism was the dominant religion of Persia, and once Georgia came under the influence of the Persian empire, the belief was introduced into the country. While Georgia was already practising Christianity at the time, chroniclers indicate that King Vakhtang Gorgasali was willing to tolerate this new religion. Today, the temple is the only one remaining.

The history of Ateshgah is murky, but sometime during the Ottoman-Persian wars of the eighteenth century, when the Turks seized Tbilisi, the temple was turned into a mosque for a time. In the years after that, Armenian families used it as an accommodation block, and residents remember people living there as recently as the 1970s.

* * *

Kldisubani St. George Church

Retrace your steps to Gomi street and continue along, with the hillside to your right. Turn down the third alley on you right, Jvaredini Turn, at the end of which is the Kldisubani St. George Church *(Map I, Point 51)*, built right up against the cliff. As with almost all of the churches in this part of town, it is on the site of a much earlier structure dating from the reign of King Vakhtang Gorgasali in the fifth century.

The current structure was built in 1753, paid for by Armenian merchant Petros Zohrabian, and then served the Armenian Christian community. In the Soviet times when religious activities were restricted, the church fell into disuse and was used to make toys. People also built small dwellings in the churchyard. After the fall of the USSR, the Georgian Orthodox authorities appropriated the church, removed all Armenian traces and restored the churchyard to its original state.

Retrace your steps back along Gomi Street. Turn right down a short lane which leads to Betlemi Street. Turn left and keep going until the junction with Asatiani Street. Turn right and keep going until you see Jvaris Mama on the left.

Jvaris Mama and Noroshen Churches

On the corner of Jerusalem Street and the main Kote Afkhazi Street is a compound containing two little churches. The smaller one is Jvaris Mama *(Map I, Point 52)*, which has an incredibly long history going back to the fifth century. This church was built in the sixteenth century and substantially renovated in 1825. The real highlight is the interior, where spectacular red, blue and gold frescoes, just recently restored, cover every square inch.

Also in the same courtyard is the slightly larger Noroshen church, built in 1793, which is currently undergoing renovation.

Kote Afkhazi Street

The main road running outside Jvaris Mama is Kote Afkhazi Street *(Map I, Point 53)*, ground-zero of all tourist related commerce in Tbilisi. Here you will find a bewildering array of cafes, bars, restaurants and souvenir shops.

The street takes its name from the prominent early twentieth-century military officer and politician. Kote Afkhazi was a Georgian nobleman who served in the Imperial Russian Tsar's army and then as a general in Georgia's national army. When the Soviets invaded, he was one of the leading players of an underground anti-Soviet resistance and led many guerilla operations. Eventually, in 1923, the Soviets caught up with him and sentenced him to death. At his execution, he reportedly said: 'I am dying with joy because I'm given the honour to be sacrificed for Georgia. My death will bring victory to Georgia!' And so his reputation as a national hero was cemented.

Gorgasali Square

Kote Afkhazi Street leads back to Gorgasali Square, which marks the end point of this route. There are lots of pleasant cafes, restaurants and bars in this area where you can rest your weary feet before starting another walking tour.

Tbilisi Walking Tour 3 - Stepping south from Gorgasali Square

This walking tour steps south of Gorgasali Square to experience sulphur baths, hidden waterfalls and the lofty battlements of Narikala Fortress.

* * *

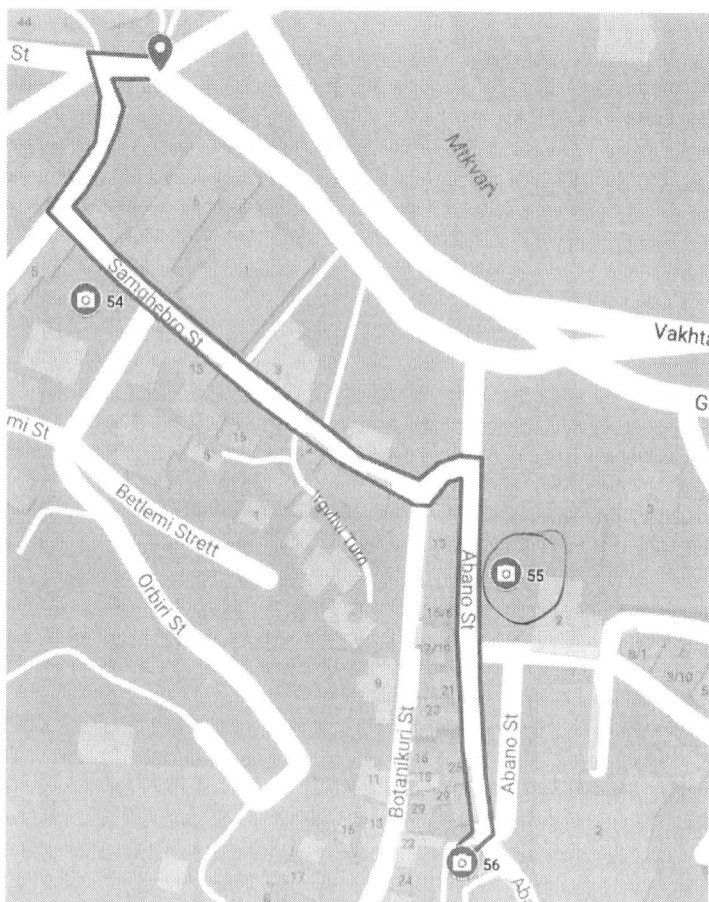

Map J: Gorgasali Square to Orbeliani Baths

Key:
54. St. George Armenian Cathedral of Tbilisi
55. Abanotubani Sulphur Baths
56. Orbeliani Baths

St. George Armenian Cathedral of Tbilisi

From Gorgasali Square, head directly south down Dzmebi Zdanevichebi Street and then take the first left along Samghebro Street. A few steps long you will see the gateway into the compound of the St. George Armenian Cathedral *(Map J, Point 54)*, which stands on a raised platform overlooking Gorgasali Square. It is one of only two still-functioning Armenian churches in Tbilisi, the other being the Ejmiatzin church on the other side of the river in the Avlabari neighbourhood. The religious authorities have since consecrated all the rest as Georgian Orthodox churches.

Among Tbilisi residents, the church is known more popularly as Tsikhisdidi, because it was built on land belonging to the prison. 'Tsikhe' in Georgian means 'prison' and 'didi' translated as 'big'. Some academics believe that the original church was built in 1251 by the wealthy Armenian merchant Umek, and as evidence point to an inscription above the Western door referring to the thirteenth century. However, the Armenian church disputes this theory and suggest instead that churches have stood on this site since 631, and that Umek 'rebuilt' rather than 'built' the church.

The cathedral has had a turbulent history and was burnt by the Persians during their 1795 invasion. As a result, most of the structure you see today dates from the eighteenth and nineteenth centuries. Inside, the frescoes mainly date from the eighteenth century, except for four large murals which were added more recently in 1923. Also look out for the tomb of Saytnova, the renowned eighteenth-century musician and artist, next to the main door.

* * *

Abanotubani Sulphur Baths

After walking back out of the cathedral, turn right and continue walking down Samghebro Street. At the end, cross over Botanikuri Street, and you'll be on Abano Street, which marks the beginning of the Abanotubani district where you can find most of Tbilisi's sulphur baths *(Map J, Point 55)*. Your nose will probably detect the rotten egg odour of the sulphur before you catch sight of the baths themselves.

Some say that it was the sulphur springs which bubble up naturally in this area which prompted King Vakhtang Gorgasali to settle here and establish Tbilisi as his capital city. In fact, the 'Tbili' part of the name roughly translates as 'warm' in Georgian. At the peak of their popularity, there were more than sixty sulphur bathhouses here, used by people to cure a variety of medical ailments and aches and pains. Today, five bathhouses remain.

Many famous travellers have enjoyed the pleasures of the baths over the years. The Russian poet Pushkin went so far as to say 'Not since my birth have I witnessed such luxuriousness as at Tbilisi baths'. French author Alexander Dumas waxed even more lyrical, asking 'Why doesn't Paris, the city of physical pleasures, have such baths?'

Directly facing you on Abano Street you see the archetypal red brick domes which cover most of the baths in this area, and in this case these are the domes of the partially subterranean Royal Bathhouse. It's a great spot for photography, with the Narikala fortress and balconied Georgian houses forming a unique backdrop to the bathhouse domes. Another popular bathhouse right next door is Gulo's Thermal Spa. Walk around this compact area, and you will find all the bathhouses and can compare prices for the usual services such as body scrubs, saunas and massages.

Continue to walk up Abano Street, and you will find the

most beautifully ornate baths on the right-hand side. These are the Orbeliani Baths *(Map J, Point 56)*, known colloquially around Tbilisi as the Blue Bathhouse, due to its magnificent blue tiled facade, designed in the style of a Persian mosque. It even has two little minarets.

As you face the Orbeliani Baths, look to your left, and you will see a narrow wooden bridge spanning the small river. Cross this and turn right along the opposite bank.

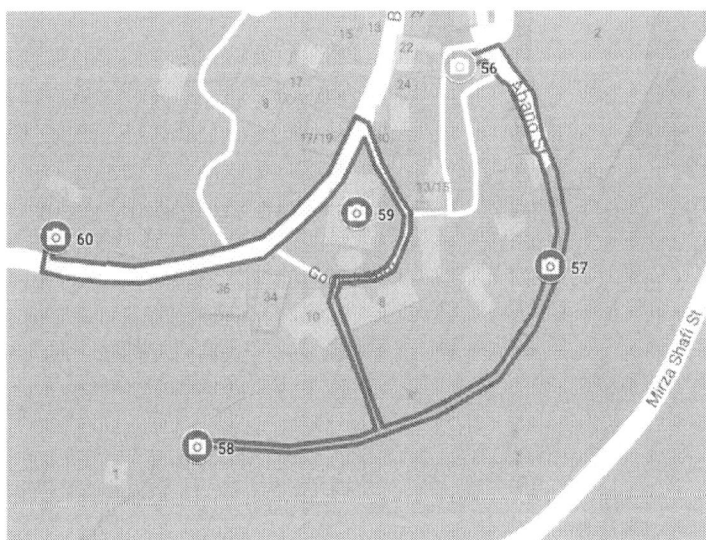

Map K: Orbeliani Baths to the Botanical Gardens

Key:
56. Orbeliani Baths
57. Leghvtakhevi
58. Dvzeli Waterfall
59. Jumah Mosque
60. Botanical Gardens

* * *

Leghvtakhevi and Dvzeli Waterfall

The small stream flowing down the centre of the narrow gorge and past all the bathhouses is the Tsavkisistskali river. Its name means 'waters of Tsavkisi' in English, and indeed the river flows through the small town of Tsavkisi west of Tbilisi. As the river flows down through this gorge and into the Mtkvari, it mingles with the waters emanating from the various sulphur springs, so the smell of rotten eggs pervades here.

As you walk up the river, the gorge narrows and deepens, and the rocky cliffs become higher and higher. Look up, and you will see balconies, and the actual old Georgian houses themselves, protruding precariously over the drop.

This gorge is called Leghvtakhevi *(Map K, Point 57)*, roughly translated as 'gorge of figs' in English, as fig trees used to be common in this area. It has only recently become accessible as a tourist attraction. Before a development project in 2012 the place was quite wild and challenging to get into; since then various walkways, bridges, kiosks and cafes have been opened, and the popularity of the area has soared with visitors and locals alike.

The path meanders along the gorge, occasionally crossing the river over small bridges. Eventually, where the cliffs are at their highest, you reach the dead end of the gorge, over which the Tsavkisistskali river tumbles in a dramatic and unexpected waterfall *(Map K, Point 58)*. It's a real hidden oasis in the middle of the city, that's nice to visit in any season. In summer, the towering cliffs and thundering waterfall cool you down, and in the winter the falls sometimes freeze into a surreal ice sculpture.

Retrace your steps back along the river away from the waterfall. After a short while, you will see a small arched stone bridge, overlooked by the multi-coloured balconies of old houses on the top of the cliff. At this point, you should climb the black wrought iron spiral staircase linking the river with the top of the cliff. A few steps through the meandering alleyways will bring you out next to the Jumah mosque.

Jumah Mosque

Tbilisi has long been a melting pot, and this extends to religion. While Georgia is overwhelmingly Orthodox Christian, there has been a remarkable tolerance of other faiths, and the Jumah mosque *(Map K, Point 59)* is on the same road as a church and a synagogue. Muslims currently constitute ten percent of the Georgian population.

The original mosque on this site dates from the 1700s, but as with many other such buildings has been victim to Tbilisi's turbulent history, and has been destroyed and rebuilt three times. The current red-brick mosque was built in 1895. It has a distinct octagonal minaret with a unique Georgian-style balcony at the top.

Unusually, Shia and Sunni Muslims pray side-by-side here, and this is due to the Soviet period of occupation. There were initially two mosques, the Jumah and the Blue mosques, where each sect prayed separately. However, in 1951, the Soviets demolished the Blue mosque to build a bridge, and as the Shias had nowhere to go. The Jumah mosque welcomed them to worship there. At first, a black curtain separated the Shias and Sunnis, but today there is no such division.

Non-Muslim visitors are welcome to go inside while adhering to the usual dress requirements and removal of shoes. The serene interior has some beautiful tiling and frescoes painted in a series of cool blues and greens.

* * *

Botanical Gardens

From the mosque, walk 100 m uphill on Botanikuri Street to reach the entrance to the National Botanical Gardens of Tbilisi *(Map K, Point 60)*. This parkland extends to just under 100 hectares and comprises 4,500 species of plant from the Caucasus and further afield. There is even a Japanese garden

There has long been some form of botanical garden in this part of Tbilisi, and records show that the predecessor of the current garden was in the lower part of the Tsavkisistskali gorge. However, Persian invaders pillaged the original garden in 1795. It was subsequently revived at today's location, with the garden receiving its formal status of National Botanical Garden in 1845.

The most popular time to visit the park is in the spring and summer when the plants are at their best. Due to the garden's size, it is best to wear comfortable walking shoes, particularly as some of the paths and trails are quite rough, and the terrain is hilly.

The next stop on this walking tour is the Narikala Fortress. There are two ways to get there.

Option 1: *After exploring the National Botanical Gardens, go back to the main entrance on Botanikuri Street. Turn up Orbiri Street on your left, which will meander up the hillside all the way up to the fortress.*

Option 2: *Within the Gardens themselves there is a path that leads up the ridge and emerges at the Kartlis Deda statue just to the west of the Fortress. However, this can be tricky to find, and signage is limited.*

* * *

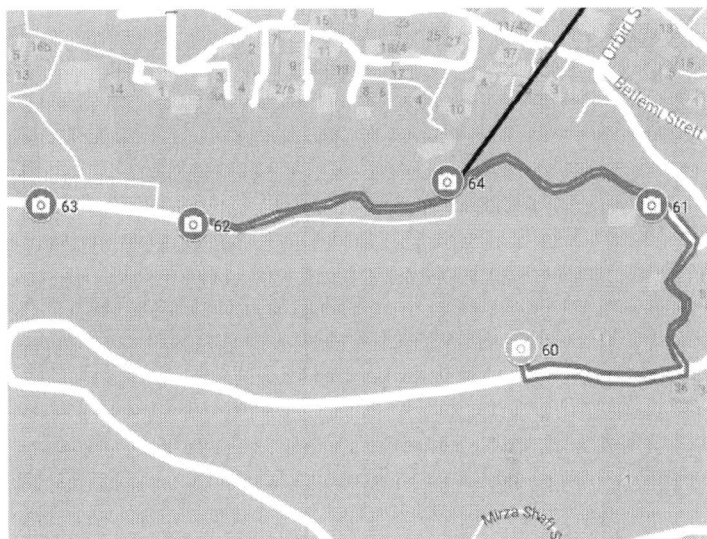

Map L: Botanical Gardens to Aerial Tram and Rike Park

Key:
> *60. Botanical Gardens*
> *61. Narikala Fortress*
> *62. Kartlis Deda*
> *63. Shahtakhti Fortress and Ivanishvili Residence*
> *64. Aerial Tram to Rike Park*

Narikala Fortress

Arrayed along the crest of the Solokai ridge, dominating the old town, is the Narikala Fortress *(Map L, Point 61)*, undoubtedly one of the most prominent of all Tbilisi's landmarks. Its strategic importance is apparent when you look at the city under you; the citadel has a panoramic view of the narrowest point of the Mtkvari river and guarded against any attack from the south. Its name means 'impregnable fortress' in English. Remarkably, it dates back more than 1700 years and as you'd expect has witnessed a long and sometimes bloody history.

The Persians laid the initial foundations for the castle in the late fourth century. When King Vakhtang Gorgasali moved his capital to Tbilisi in the next century, he immediately recognised the importance of the Persian fortifications, and he set about enlarging and strengthening them. The next set of occupiers, the Arabs, continued this theme of continually improving the defences, and almost all of the ruined walls you see today are the result of their labours. In the centuries after that, waves of invaders, including Mongolians, Turks and Persians, all left their mark on the structure.

If you are approaching from Orbiri Street, you will first meet a small square tower, through which there is a roughly-hewn gateway. At the top of the steep cobbled path, you will enter the lower court of the fortress, at the centre of which is the St. Nicholas church. While taking the form of a traditional 'inscribed' cross design, this is pretty much brand new, having been built in 1996-7 to replace the destroyed thirteenth-century original. From here you can then explore the battlements of the fortress west along the ridge. Some of the walls have been extensively restored, such as those surrounding St. Nicholas Church, whereas others have been untouched for centuries.

Kartlis Deda

Eventually, you will pass the cable car station, and about 200 m further on is the imposing and somewhat space-age Kartlis Deda *(Map L, Point 62)*, or Mother of Georgia statue. This 20 m high woman is designed to represent the Georgian character. She holds a sword in one hand, demonstrating the Georgian's passionate defence of their homeland over the centuries; in the other, she offers a bowl of wine, showing the country's hospitable and welcoming nature. Leading Georgian sculptor Elguja Amashukeli designed the statue, which was erected in 1958 when the city celebrated its 1500th anniversary. Kartlis Deda is now undoubtedly Georgia's most recognised woman and has become a national symbol.

Shahtakhti Fortress and Ivanishvili Residence

Moving past Mother Georgia are the ruins of the Shahtakhti Fortress *(Map L, Point 63)*, which was used as an observatory by the Arabs in the seventh to ninth centuries. Finally, at the extreme western edge of the ridge is the gargantuan residence of Bidzina Ivanishvili, resembling something out of a Bond movie with its helipads and futuristic architecture. Ivanishvili is one of Georgia's wealthiest men and served as the country's prime minister in 2012-13.

Now retrace your steps back to the cable car station.

Aerial Tram

One of Tbilisi's newer attractions, just built in 2012, the aerial tram *(Map L, Point 64)* connects Narikala Fortress with the Rike Park just across the river from Gorgasali Square. To ride on it, you need to use a Metromoney card. If you don't already have one, they cost 2 GEL and can be used on any bus and metro in the city. The one-way tram journey then costs 2.50 GEL.

During the ride, you get spectacular views of the entire old town, Mtkvari river, the Bridge of Peace, Rike Park and the Presidential Palace. The lower cable car terminus is inside Rike Park.

Rike Park

Popular with residents and visitors alike, Rike Park stretches along the river from the Presidential Palace to Metekhi Bridge. The most prominent feature within the park is the Concert Hall and Exhibition Centre. This gleaming metallic building has a smooth, tubular design comprising two wings. The northern part is designed to be a music hall seating more than five hundred concertgoers, while the southern portion is an exhibition venue.

Winding paths and picturesque landscaping connect other highlights such as a children's maze, outsized chess boards, dancing fountains and various quirky sculptures one of which is a giant piano. Under the cliff, over which balconies jut out precariously, is a variety of restaurants, and down on the river bank itself are yet more cafes and bars, perfect for a well-earned rest at the end of a day touring Tbilisi.

A short walk across the Metekhi Bridge sees you back in Gorgasali Square where this walking tour ends.

Tbilisi Walking Tour 4 - Exploring east of the Mtkvari River

This walking tour takes in the sights to the east of the Mtkvari river and begins in the rather grand Marjanishvili Square.

This route can continue from the 'Navigating North from Freedom Square' walking tour. Simply take a red line metro train, one stop from Rustaveli Square in the direction of Akhmeteli Theatre and get off at the Marjanishvili Square station. Or, for those with more time, do the tour on a different day, taking a metro from the station nearest your hotel.

* * *

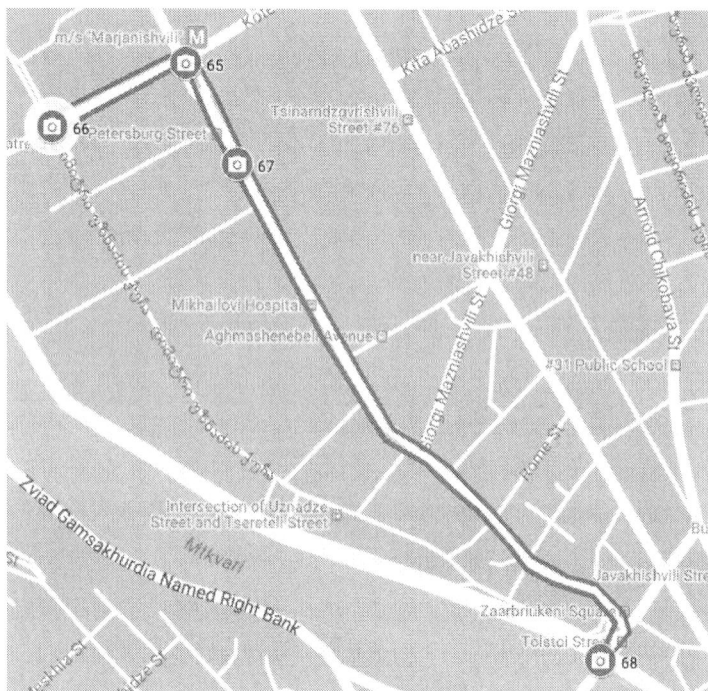

Map M: Marjanishvili Square to Dry Bridge Market

Key:
   65. Marjanishvili Square
   66. Marjanishvili Theatre
   67. Davit Aghmashenebeli Street
   68. Dry Bridge Market

Marjanishvili Square

Marjanishvili Square *(Map M, Point 65)* is at the heart of the area developed by German colonists during the nineteenth century, and glancing at a map, you will notice how the streets here are laid out on a strict grid layout in true Teutonic style. The square takes its name from Kote Marjanishvili, the celebrated Georgian theatre director famous for his extravagant productions. His theatre is just one block down the road from the square along Marjanishvili Street. By now you should see just how revered this director is, from the number of high profile places named after him.

Walk 150 m down Marjanishvili Street southwest towards the river.

Marjanishvili Theatre

Marjanishvili Theatre *(Map M, Point 66)* is one of the oldest and most important in the country. It was established in 1928 by Kote Marjanishvili in the town of Kutaisi in western Georgia but moved shortly after that to Tbilisi in 1930. It occupied a building that used to be a philanthropic public library set up by the successful merchant brothers Zubaliashvili. Almost a century later the theatre is still going strong. The facade of the theatre is classic art nouveau, and the inside also reflects the iconic designs of the early part of the twentieth century. The main auditorium has seating for more than six hundred people. While almost all productions are in Georgian, the theatre has recently started providing occasional English subtitles for plays. You can check the latest playbill at www.marjanishvili.com/en.

Walk back to Marjanishvili Square and turn right along Davit Aghmashenebeli Street.

Davit Aghmashenebeli Street

This thoroughfare is the main commercial street to the east of the Mtkvari river and handsome, recently-renovated nineteenth-century buildings run along its length *(Map M, Point 67)*. It runs from the area near the Tbilisi Central railway station to Saarbrucken Square.

The street takes its name from the twelfth-century King David IV, popularly known as David the Builder due to his massive construction projects. It is one of the most frequented shopping streets in the whole of Tbilisi and has just undergone a comprehensive revamp. Consequently, most of the buildings lining the street are now sparkling and beautifully-maintained, and the walk along its length is a pleasant stroll indeed.

Halfway along the street, look out for the striking neo-gothic facade of the Mikhailovi Hospital at number 60. Directly opposite the hospital, at number 61, is the old Soviet Propaganda Centre, a 1970s brutalist concrete structure, sporting a colourful mosaic designed by Zurab Tsereteli.

As you approach the end of the street, it becomes pedestrianised. Here, beautiful old balconied buildings line the road, and pavement cafes and bars proliferate. You eventually emerge onto the cobbled Saarbrucken Square at the eastern end of the Saarbrucken bridge.

Dry Bridge Market

Cross Saarbrucken Bridge and you will straight away begin to notice the merchants of the Dry Bridge Market *(Map M,*

Point 68). For anyone who loves a bargain, this is a must-visit place in Tbilisi. Here you can pick up an authentic and quirky souvenir of Georgia, often dating back into Soviet times and beyond. Some people regard this market as a kind of open-air museum, as you see relics of the Soviet era you don't usually see elsewhere.

People love browsing these stalls for old coins, kitchenware, books, vinyl records, vintage appliances and phones, postcards, and just about anything else you can imagine. Negotiation is the order of the day, and as stall holders don't often speak English, a few words of Georgian or Russian would come in handy to make sure you secure a bargain.

The market is open every day, from 10 am to 5 pm, although traders may pack up early in the case of severe weather.

From Saarbrucken Square to St Trinity Cathedral is around 1.5 km, and a short, cheap taxi ride away.

Alternatively, to see a bit more of this part of Tbilisi you can easily walk, although there are some quite long uphill sections. Walk along Leo Tolstoy Street then turn right down Kosta Khetagurovi Street. Continue along the river until you reach the statue of Baratashvili. Climb the steps to the left onto Elene Akhvalediani rise. Walk to the end, turn left and then continue until you reach the cathedral.

* * *

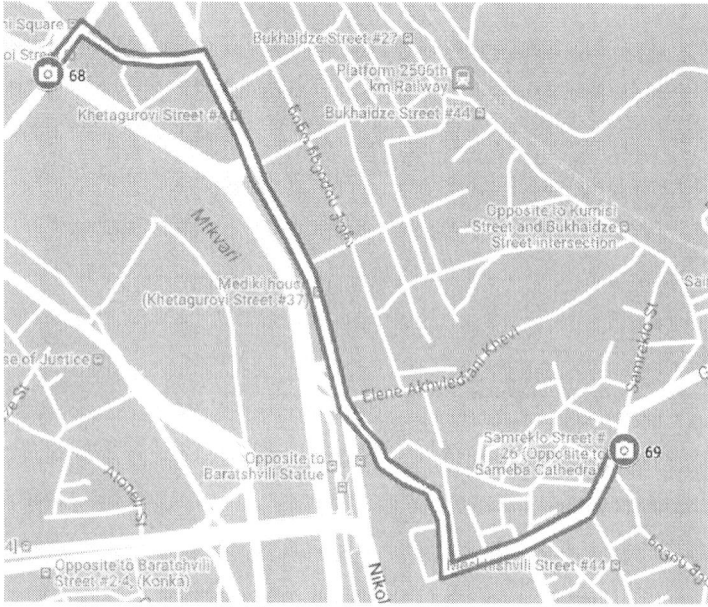

Map N: Dry Bridge Market to St Trinity Cathedral

Key:
  68. Dry Bridge Market
  69. Trinity Cathedral

St. Trinity (Samebo) Cathedral

St. Trinity, also known as Samebo, is the primary cathedral in Tbilisi for the Georgian orthodox religion *(Map N, Point 69)*. It was completed in 2004 and was built to commemorate 1500 years of the Georgian Orthodox church, and 2000 years since the birth of Christ. With an area of 5000 square metres, it is one of the largest religious buildings in the world. An even the bells are monumental; there is a group of nine with the biggest weighing in at a hefty eight tons.

Its situation at the top of the hill in the Avlabari district means that the church is visible from far and wide. It is built in a traditional Georgian Orthodox style, although it is stretched vertically to a more than 100 m height, giving it a more towering perspective. Opinions are divided, and some regard it as something of an eyesore by some, while others view it as an architectural triumph. You'll have to make your own mind up when you get there.

Inside, the dome is supported by eight impressive columns that appear to reach all the way up to heaven. While not too ornate, you should look out for the beautiful gilded icons that are scattered throughout. There are nine individual chapels each dedicated to a particular saint, some of which are underground. The deepest foundations of the structure include holy materials such as rocks from Mount Sion and the Jordan River, and soil from Jerusalem and St. George's tomb.

The cathedral is just one part of a sprawling complex comprising the residence of the patriarch, a monastery, a separate free-standing belfry, theology school, workshops and even a hotel.

From the cathedral entrance, turn left down Samreko Street and then turn left along Lado Meskhishvili Street. Follow this street all the way to Avlabari Square. Walk to your left across the square, where you will see the sculpture to the actors of Mimino.

* * *

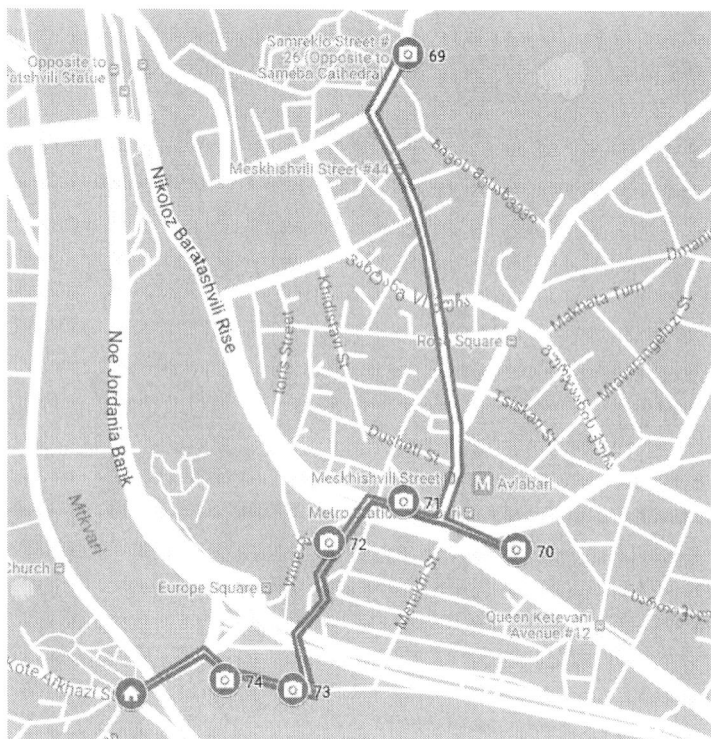

Map O: St Trinity Cathedral to Gorgasali Square

Key:

69. *Trinity Cathedral*
70. *Sculpture to the Actors of Mimino*
71. *Ejmiadzin Armenian Church*
72. *Queen Darejan's (Sachino) Palace*
73. *Metekhi Cathedral*
74: *King Gorgasali Statue*

Sculpture to the Actors of Mimino

Just across Avlabari Square from the Ejmiadzin church is a whimsical statue celebrating the characters of Mimino *(Map O, Point 70)*, a much-loved 1970s comedy film, written by the very same Revaz Gabriadze who later opened his puppet theatre in Tbilisi. In the movie, a Georgian bush helicopter pilot, Mimino, who dreams of a high-flying airline job, goes to Moscow to pursue his dream. There he meets an Armenian truck driver who was mistakenly lodged at his hotel, and together they have lots of adventures. Eventually, Mimino gets a job flying the Tu144 supersonic jet flying all over the world. However, he ultimately succumbs to homesickness and comes back to the bosom of his family and friends in Georgia.

The sculpture was created by Zurab Tsereteli, the Georgian-born painter and sculptor who founded MoMA Tbilisi.

Walk back across Avlabari Square to the Ejmiadzin Armenian church, which will be facing you.

Ejmiadzin Armenian Church

This Armenian Apostolic church *(Map O, Point 71)* was built in 1804 to serve the local Armenian community. Today, it is one of only two operating Armenian churches in the city, the other being the St. George Armenian cathedral just behind Gorgasali Square.

The church is mostly built from red brick and has a

distinctive white drum and dome. Inside, the walls have mostly been whitewashed. To the east of the church, at the end nearest to the metro station, is a superior example of a khachkar, or Armenian stele, showing a carved cross and many elaborate floral motifs. To the side of the church is a curious tall plinth upon which is a small bowler-hatted bust. This statue is a monument to Alexander Mantasgev, a prominent Armenian oil tycoon and philanthropist.

The church was recently the epicentre of an international controversy which blew up from the most trivial beginnings. According to the Georgians, a Georgian woman complained that an Armenian priest's car had blocked her own. When some other Georgians tried to help her, several Armenians attacked them. The Armenians side, however, claimed that the woman verbally and racially abused the Armenians. Fifty people were involved in the clashes. Afterwards, the local Armenian diocese complained, resulting in the Armenian foreign office demanding that the Georgians investigate the 'hate crime'. Some Georgian commentators believe that such overreactions are the result of long-held tensions which were re-ignited following the construction of the St. Trinity Cathedral over part of an old Armenian cemetery.

From the Ejmiadzin Armenian Church, cross the main road. As you dive into the narrow alleyways, take as your landmark the rounded dome and steeple of the Church of the Transfiguration in Queen Darejan's Palace.

Queen Darejan's (Sachino) Palace

The Palace of Queen Darejan *(Map O, Point 72)* is otherwise known as Sachino Palace. Sachino in Georgian means conspicuous, and this proves to be an apt name considering its prominent position overlooking the Mtkheti river and the city. The palace was built in 1776 by King Erekle II on the remnants of the older Alvlabar fortress walls, some of which are still visible today, and the queen used it as a summer residence.

There are two main surviving elements of the complex. The first is a dramatic pavilion perched right on the highest point of the old fortress walls. Circular in shape, the pavilion has a vertigo-inducing wrap-around balcony, from which there are stunning panoramic views of Tbilisi's old town. The second is the Church of the Transfiguration, built at the same time as the palace in 1776. The church has a distinctive tower with an exposed belfry topped by a rounded dome and steeple. While it was used as the private chapel for the Royals, it now serves the whole community.

Queen Darejan was the third wife of King Erekle II, and remarkably their marriage lasted forty-eight years and produced a staggering twenty-three children. She became quite involved in politics and was opposed to the continuing rapprochement with Russia. When her husband died in 1798, her stepson George XII became the new king. George actively sought Russian protection for Georgia and so ratcheted up the conflict with his stepmother. These tensions escalated to such a degree that he confined Darejan to the Sachino Palace. After George died in 1800, the Russians forbade the nomination of a new monarch, prompting Queen Darejan and her sons into open rebellion. Eventually, Tsar Alexander I ordered the deportation of the entire royal family. The queen was deported to Russia in 1803. Following her departure, the site was redeveloped as a monastery and then as a seminary for the children of ecclesiastics.

From the palace, narrow paths will leading to stone staircases descending down the hill towards the river. The steps will eventually emerge near the Metekhi Cathedral.

Metekhi Cathedral

The Metekhi district is on a clifftop plateau on the eastern side of the Mtkvari river. It's one of the oldest neighbourhoods of Tbilisi. It is said that King Vakhtang first erected a palace and church here in the fifth century and that a Georgian saint, Shushanik, was also buried here. All of these structures were wiped out by thirteenth-century Mongol raiders.

The church you see today *(Map O, Point 73)* was built just after this turbulent period, around 1280. As with most other historical structures in the city, it has been damaged and subsequently renovated many times over. It's a small miracle that the church has survived at all, given that in the Soviet era the communist leader of Georgia, the infamous Lavrenti Beria, proposed to demolish the church. These plans luckily never came to fruition.

The plan of the church is a cross-cupola design, the dominant form of churches in the Middle Ages, particularly in this region. As with the Jvari Monastery just outside of Tbilisi, the spaces between the arms of the cross are filled in, producing a square ground plan. Exterior ornamentation is quite sparse, with architectural flourishes limited to around the windows. Inside, the church has a real atmosphere of antiquity, with its roughly hewn stone walls, icons, and flickering candles. At the weekend, you may be lucky to see a baptism or wedding ceremony.

King Gorgasali Statue

Next to Metekhi Cathedral is the imposing statue of King Vakhtang Gorgasali *(Map O, Point 74)*, gazing sternly out across the river and old town Tbilisi. This is a fitting end to this walking tour as King Gorgasali is widely credited with founding Tbilisi way back in the fifth century, and many other towns, castles, monasteries and churches.

King Gorgasali is one of the most popular characters from Georgia's long history, and has even been canonised by the Georgian Orthodox Church. He is the subject of epic poems and legends, all of which extol his greatness and courage.

This particular statue of the king, high up on the Metekhi clifftop, was installed in 1967, and designed by Elguja Amashukeli - the sculpter also responsible for the equally formidable Kartlis Deda.

From King Gorgasali's statue, stroll back across metekhi Bridge to Gorgasali Square, where this walking tour comes to an end.

Day Trips from Tbilisi

The UNESCO World Heritage Sites of Mtskheta make for a comfortable half-day trip from Tbilisi. The easiest way to get there would be to hire a taxi, and there is no shortage of willing drivers who would be more than happy to take you out there! Of course, negotiate the price before you get in, but depending on your negotiating skills you should be able to get a ride there and back for USD 15-20.

A cheaper alternative is to get a marshrutka. First, take a metro to Didube station. Next to this is the bus station, where you can find the marshrutka. You will need to buy a ticket at the cashier. While this is an excellent option for going to Mtskheta itself, the Jvari Monastery is on a relatively remote hilltop and would require an additional taxi ride to and from town.

If you would like to make a full day trip, you can go around another fifty minutes past Mtskheta to Gori, where there are ancient sites of interest and the Stalin Museum.

— Mtskheta —

Mtskheta, a mere 20 km north of Tbilisi, is an ancient city that has played a central role throughout much of Georgia's existence. In recognition of this religious and historical significance, its monuments, notably the Svetitskhoveli Cathedral and Jvaris Monastery, have been UNESCO World Heritage Sites since 1994. Recently, in 2014, the Georgian Orthodox Church declared Mtskheta a 'Holy City'. Any visit to Tbilisi would not be complete without a day trip here.

The city was the long-time capital of the Georgian Kingdom of Iberia, from the third century BC onwards. It was where Christianity was adopted as the state religion, following St. Nino's conversion of the ruling king in 327 AD. In the sixth century, King Dachi, the successor to King Vakhtang Gorgasali, moved the capital to Tbilisi as it was more readily defended from invaders. Mtskheta nevertheless remained as the headquarters of the Georgian Orthodox Church, and every Georgian king was coronated and buried here, up to the end of the monarchy in the nineteenth century.

The natural setting of Mtskheta is also a draw. It sits in a valley at the confluence of the Mtkvari and Aragvi rivers, surrounded by hilly country. There are lots of old cobbled streets to explore and balconied houses to admire. In the town square outside the cathedral, there are some decent cafes and restaurants, and you can walk lunch off with a pleasant stroll down to the tranquil Mtkvari river.

— Svetitskhoveli Cathedral —

The eleventh-century Svetitskhoveli Cathedral is a masterpiece of Georgian religious medieval architecture. It is said to be the burial site of the robe, known as the mantle, that Christ wore during the crucifixion. The cathedral is undoubtedly the holiest place in Georgia and attracts pilgrims from all over the Caucasus.

In Georgia, 'Sveti' means 'pillar' and 'tskhoveli' translates as 'life-giving'. To find out why the church takes this name we have to look back to the first century AD when a Georgian Jew called Elias visited Jerusalem at the time of Jesus' crucifixion. He bought the robe of Jesus from a soldier and returned to his homeland. When his sister, Sidonia, touched it, she dropped dead from the extreme emotions she felt. She wouldn't let go of the robe, even in death, and so she was buried with it, on the site where the cathedral stands today.

After that, the grave stood alone without any religious buildings erected around it. However, a huge cedar tree grew from her grave, and in the fourth century King Merian, the first king to be converted to Christianity by St. Nino, ordered seven columns to be made, to build a church. The seventh column turned out to have magical powers and rose into the air, and the saint had to pray all night before it came back down to earth. Subsequently, some people spoke of a holy liquid emanating from the pillar which cured any disease, so giving rise to the name Svetitskhoveli. When in the cathedral, look out for the second column upon which a nineteenth-century icon illustrates this story, with Sidonia and an angel lifting the column, and King Miran in the foreground.

The original fourth-century church was built from wood and was superceded in the fifth century by a more sturdy stone structure, the excavated foundations of which are alongside the present-day cathedral.

The cathedral is perfectly proportioned, soaring above the low-lying village of Mtskheta. It is cross-shaped, as you'd expect, with a dome on a tall drum. The structure appears to comprise of a series of stone waves, with the porch, lower nave and upper nave getting progressively higher towards the drum. While the stonework is relatively unadorned, different colours are used for various structural elements;

walls are mostly yellow stone, the drum is green, while red stone appears around the apse window. Look out for wine leaf motifs on the western facade as you approach the main entrance. Curiously, on the northern facade, there is a carving of a hand holding a bevel square, allegedly the hand of the architect, Arsukidze. Legend has it that the architect's teacher was so jealous of his masterpiece at Svetitskhoveli that he had his hand chopped off. An inscription on the eastern facade confirms that Arsukidze did not live long enough to see the church completed, but the cause of his death is not known for sure. King Herekle II built the high defensive walls surrounding the cathedral compound in the eighteenth century.

You enter the cathedral from the western door. Immediately on your right is a fourth-century baptismal font, purportedly used for the baptism of King Mirian. Walking down the nave, on the right side, is what appears to be a small stone church. It is a thirteenth-century copy of the Chapel of Christ's Sepulchre in Jerusalem, built to symbolise the position of Svetitskhoveli as the second most holy place in the Christian world due to the presence of Jesus' mantle. In front of the chapel is the grave of Sidonius where fragments of the seventh column remain.

Frescoes originally covered the inside of the cathedral, yet most of these did not survive. In the 1830's Russian authorities whitewashed over them to give the church a 'tidier' look in advance of a planned visit by Tsar Nicholas I which eventually didn't even happen. Today, restoration projects are trying to uncover these, and you can see some thirteenth-century frescoes depicting the 'Beast of the Apocalypse' and various Zodiac figures. The other frescoes and icons visible today mostly date from the nineteenth and twentieth centuries.

Svetitskhoveli played host to all the coronations and royal

burials during Georgia's time as a kingdom. Ten kings are believed to have been buried here, but so far only three graves have been found, all arrayed before the altar. The most prominent of these is the tomb of King Vakhtang Gorgasali, fronted with many devotional candles. The eighteenth century King Herekle II is alongside, identified by its sword and shield, and next to his grave is his son King Giorgi XII, the very last king of Georgia.

The cathedral is open daily from 8 am to 10 pm.

— Jvari Monastery —

As with many of the most celebrated ancient churches of Georgia, the Jvari Monastery is perched high up on the top of a small mountain. The sixth-century structure is one of the most visited and photographed in Georgia, and along with other prominent sites down in Mtskheta has been listed as a UNESCO World Heritage Site.

The monastery can trace its origins way back to the fourth century, at which point we meet St Nino again (we saw a replica of her grapevine cross in the Sioni Cathedral in Tbilisi). The saint converted the then-king of the area, Mirian the Third, to Christianity, and afterwards erected a cross on top of the mountain where Jvari monastery now stands. The cross was said to perform miracles, and pilgrims soon came pouring in from all over the Caucasus. In 545, the faithful erected a small church over the remaining fragments of the cross, and the present-day building replaced this in 590. Unusually for historic structures in Georgia, the monastery has by and large escaped the ravages of history, other than some minor damage incurred by Arab raiders in the tenth century. Today, Jvari is very much an active religious site, and on the weekends you might be lucky enough to witness a Georgian wedding ceremony or baptism.

Its design was a first-of-its-kind. While the church's plan is cruciform, the spaces between the arms of the cross shape are filled in with little chapels, making an almost square ground plan. These well-balanced proportions evoke a feeling of tranquillity and harmony, emphasised through the general lack of excessive ornamentation. Outside, the stonework has little carving or other embellishments, although there is a particularly fine bas-relief of angels holding a cross above the south door. Inside the walls are almost entirely bare, making the church feel more spacious and lofty than it actually is.

The classic 1840 poem, the *Mtsyri*, by the celebrated Russian writer Mikhail Lermontov, immortalised the Jvari Monastery. It was supposedly based on a true story he heard during his time serving in the Caucasus as an army officer, whereby a general captured a six-year-old Circassian Muslim boy and left him with Georgian monks at Jvari Monastery.

In its final version, the poem describes the situation of the monastery:

At that place, where
  The streams, Aragvi and Kura,
  Embracing as two sisters,
  Flow together with a roar,
  There was a monastery.

The boy found it hard to get used to life in the monastery but seemingly reconciled himself to his fate. Secretly, however, he had never given up hope of seeing his family again, and one day fled the monastery. He spent three days wandering the valley lost, and in the end is found just near the monastery having walked in a big circle. He dies soon afterwards. Mtsyri means novice monk, and the poem shows that the boy, who perished after leaving the monastery, has proved to be just that and no longer Circassian. In other words, nurture, or culture, has prevailed over the boy's nature.

The monastery was built right on the very edge of a vertical cliff, and there is a spectacular view which features on most Georgian postcards. Down below in the valley there is the iconic confluence of the Mtkvari and Aragvi rivers, and nestling in the centre is Svetitskhoveli Cathedral surrounded by Mtskheta.

The site is open daily between 9 am and 10 pm.

— Gori —

Depending on your interest in the history of the Soviet Union, you might consider an extension to the usual Mtskheta day trip. The town of Gori, famed as the birthplace of Joesph Stalin, is less than an hour's drive away, west along the E60 motorway.

Stalin Museum

Remarkably, considering twentieth-century history, and in particular Georgia's repression during the USSR time, the Stalin Museum has remained as a shrine to the infamous dictator. First opened in 1957 shortly after his death, the museum is next door to the house where Stalin was born in 1878.

With its heavy, oppressive concrete structure, the museum itself shouts Stalinism. Once you are inside the main entrance, you know that you will have an experience unlike any other. A grand marble staircase leads up to an imposing statue of the man himself. The rooms housing the various exhibits are authentically Soviet in decor and ambience.

The artefacts on display are mostly personal items such as the last packet of cigarettes Stalin smoked and his preferred winter coat. Various paintings and photographs document his eventful life. Perhaps the darkest display in the museum, and one most likely to give you nightmares, is Stalin's death mask mounted in a dimly and eerily lit chamber. In the yard of the museum is Stalin's personal train carriage and his childhood house. There is no mention anywhere in the museum of purges, gulags or any other murderous practices.

The museum is open daily between 10 am and 6 pm, and the entrance fee is 15 GEL.

Gori Fortress

Dominating the whole town is the Gori Fortress, an impressive thirteenth-century castle high up on a nearby hill. Due to its strategic importance, it naturally attracted the attention of all invading armies and was captured by the Ottomans in the sixteenth century. After that, it continually changed hands between the Turks, Georgians and Persians. From the battlements are spectacular views of Gori and the Caucasus in the distance.

Due to many battles for control of the castle, much of it has repeatedly been destroyed and then rebuilt. The remaining structure you see dates from the seventeenth and eighteenth centuries, with some of the more visible damage caused by a 1920 earthquake.

Gori was on the frontline yet again in 2008, when Russian forces occupied the town during its brief invasion of Georgia. In the northeast part of the castle, you can see a sculpture of a circle of mutilated fighters as a memorial to those who lost their lives.

Uplistsikhe cave complex

Uplistsikhe is one of the oldest settlements anywhere in Georgia, founded three thousand years ago in the late Bronze Age. It became an important political and religious centre, and its prominence lasted well into the twelfth century.

Today the remains of the cave complex spread over 40,000 square metres, with the central area containing most of the rock-hewn structures. In addition to regular caves used for accommodation, you can also visit caves used as bakeries, pharmacies, places of sacrifice and even a prison, all connected by tunnels.

Archaeologists have found out that in the pre-Christian era Uplistsikhe residents were engaged in sun worship, and have unearthed many such temples. Upon the introduction of Christianity, the importance of the cave complex dwindled somewhat but continued nonetheless.

Its second heyday came when the Arabs captured Tbilisi, and the Kings of Kartli made Uplistsikhe their residence. Accordingly, the stature of the settlement grew, and it eventually counted 20,000 residents. When Georgians wrestled back control of Tbilisi, Uplistsikhe immediately went into a decline from which it never recovered.

Uplistsikhe is on the tentative list for inclusion on the UNESCO World Heritage Program. So now is the perfect time to visit, before it gains full status and the crowds of tourists start to appear.

Preparing for your visit to Tbilisi

— Essential info —

When to Visit

Tbilisi is affected by both continental and subtropical influences. However, as it is bounded by mountain ranges, particularly in the north, it is sheltered from harsh winter weather. The city has a reasonably mild microclimate, and rainfall is spread pretty evenly throughout the year.

Generally, spring and autumn in Tbilisi are cool and pleasant. Summer temperatures are between 20C and 30C but can top 40C in the middle of the day. Winters are cold, and snow falls between 15-25 days each winter.

Visas

Georgia has a relatively relaxed visa regime. More than ninety nationalities are visa-exempt, including those from all

EU countries, the US, Canada, Gulf countries, South Africa, Australia, New Zealand and selected southeast Asian and central and South American countries. Many others can apply for an e-visa online from the official Georgia e-Visa Portal, www.evisa.gov.ge. The cost is USD 20 plus a 2% service fee, and it takes around five working days to process. For all other nationalities, it is necessary to apply for a visa in advance at a Georgian embassy.

Currency

The currency is the Georgian Lari (GEL). Each Lari splits into 100 Tetri. At the time of writing, April 2018, one US Dollar bought 2.40 Lari, one British Pound bought 3.39 Lari, and one Euro got 2.96 Lari. You can easily exchange these main currencies in the city, and exchanges and banks are commonplace. ATMs also accept Visa, Visa Electron, Mastercard and Maestro cards.

Time Zone

Tbilisi is in the Georgia Standard Time (GET) zone, which is GMT+4. The country does not currently observe daylight savings time.

Electricity

Georgia's electricity is of the 220V/50Hz variety. The wall sockets take plugs with two round pins. Take a range of adaptors with you to make sure you can connect.

— Getting There and Away —

By Air

Tbilisi has one airport serving all international and national airlines. Tbilisi International Airport (TBS) is about a 17 km drive southeast of the city centre. It offers a wide range of routes spanning the Middle East, Europe and Russia.

Here are the airlines currently connecting **international destinations** with Tbilisi:

- Aegean Airlines flies to Athens three times each week. www.aegeanair.com.
- Aeroflot has double daily flights to Moscow Sheremetyevo, with onward connections on its services and those of the SkyTeam Alliance. www.aeroflot.com
- Air Arabia links Tbilisi with Sharjah 10 times per week. www.airarabia.com
- Air Astana flies to Almaty and Astana. www.airastana.com
- Air Baltic goes to Riga three times a week.
- Azerbaijan Airlines flies to Baku twice daily. www.azal.az.
- Belavia has daily service to Minsk. www.belavia.by.
- China Southern flies to Urumqi three times a week. www.csair.com
- El Al links Tbilisi with Tel Aviv three times a week. www.elal.com.
- FlyDubai offers flights four flights a day to its Dubai

hub, with onward connections around the Middle East, Africa, the Subcontinent and Europe. www.flydubai.com. Alternatively, passengers can connect to Emirates' global network.

- Georgian Airways offers the widest selection of destinations from Tbilisi, including Amsterdam, Athens, Barcelona, Beirut, Berlin, Bologna, Bratislava, Brussels, Cologne, Kazan, Kiev, London Gatwick, Moscow Vnukovo, Paris Charles de Gaulle, Tel Aviv, Vienna and Yerevan. www.georgian-airways.com.

- Gulf Air goes to Bahrain three times weekly. www.gulfair.com.

- LOT has daily flights to Warsaw with onward connections throughout Europe. www.lot.com.

- Lufthansa has daily flights to Munich. www.lufthansa.com

- Iran Air www.iranair.com, Iran Aseman Airlines www.iaa.ir and Qeshm Airlines www.qeshm-air.com all fly to Tehran, Iran.

- Israir flies to Tel Aviv three times a week. www.israir.co.il

- Pegasus Airlines has daily flights To Istanbul Sabha Gokcen airport. www.flypgs.com.

- Qatar Airways has daily flights to its hub at Doha, from where you can connect to its global network. One of these daily flights also stops off at Baku. www.qatarairways.com

- S7 flies to Moscow Domodedovo. www.s7.ru

- Turkish Airlines has a flight to Istanbul four times most days. From its Istanbul hub, you can fly just about anywhere in the world. www.turkishairlines.com

- Ukraine International Airlines flies to Kiev. www.flyuia.com.

- Ural Airlines serves Yekaterinburg twice a week and Moscow Zhukovsky four times weekly. www.uralairlines.com
- Wataniya links Tbilisi with Kuwait four times a week. www.wataniyaairways.com

As Georgia is quite a small country, there are no air services to other cities domestically.

By Rail

There is a relatively extensive railway network in Georgia, comprising just over 1500 km of track and 22 passenger stations. This comprises a main line running from the Russian border in the northwest to the Azerbaijani border in the southeast, with various lines branching off to major population centres. The most modern double-decker electric trains run between Batumi to Tbilisi. The fare is unlikely to exceed more than USD 15 anywhere in the country.

Tbilisi is connected to several international destinations such as Baku in Azerbaijan and Yerevan in Armenia. In Kupe class, a one-way fare to Yerevan should be around USD 30, and USD 20 to Baku. There is a link to Kars in Turkey, from which the extensive Turkish railway network can be accessed, with connections on to Europe. To travel to destinations in Russia, it is necessary to transit in Baku, as the security situation in Abkhazia has led to the closure of the railway in the border region.

Tickets can be purchased online on the Georgian Railways website, www.railway.ge, although the online booking functionality appears to be only in Georgian. The site also has full timetable and route information, displayed in English. As an alternative, visit the English language ticket booking engine at https://tkt.ge/en/Railway, where you can buy domestics tickets with foreign credit cards.

By Road

There are easy border crossings with Turkey, Azerbaijan and Armenia. Travelling from Russia is more problematic due to the security situations in South Ossetia and Abkhazia.

From Turkey, there are two primary crossings. The first one is at Sarpi on the Black Sea coast and is handy for travellers going to Batumi, a mere 15 km from the border. The other at Vale is more convenient for Tbilisi.

From Azerbaijan, there are two main border crossings. The most direct route from Baku is through the 'Red Bridge' immigration post, a short 70 km drive from Tbilisi. The other option is the Lagodekhi crossing in the extreme east of Georgia.

From Armenia, the southeastern border post at Sadakhlo is conveniently placed on the direct route between Yerevan and Tbilisi. An alternative crossing is at Bavra in southern Georgia.

Travelling from Russia presents more of a challenge. The most straightforward option is to cross the border at Stepantsminda in the Kazbegi National Park. Some travellers report a smooth transit, whereas others are questioned at length by the Russian authorities. So you should be prepared for both scenarios!

By Boat

The main ports of Georgia are Batumi and Poti, and from

both there are regular services to Ukraine and Bulgaria.

Ukrferry, www.ukrferry.com, links both Georgian ports with Chornomorsk in southern Ukraine. Large ro-ro ferries operate twice a week in both directions, with the voyage taking about 48 hours. A basic berth costs USD 110 one-way.

There is also an interesting route from Bulgaria, operated by Navibulgar, www.navbul.com, under the brand FerrySped. Their ferry links Poti with Varna, usually once per week. The journey takes 54 hours, and a basic berth costs EUR 110 one-way.

Batumi is linked by fast hydrofoils to Sochi in Russia, by the Express Batumi shipping company. However, this is currently limited to Russians and nationals of other CIS countries.

— Getting Around —

From the airport

Bus 37 runs a service at 12-minute intervals from the airport to the city centre all day from 7 am to 11 pm. Stops include the Rustaveli and Avlabari metro stations and Freedom Square. The fare is 0.50 GED. However, if you are travelling with a lot of luggage, this might not be the best option.

There is an impressive new railway station just a few metres away from the terminal. However, the schedule is quite minimal with infrequent trains in the morning and evening rush hours. The Tbilisi Airport website, www.tbilisiairport.com, has the latest timings.

As most visitors' flights arrive at anti-social hours in the early morning, taking a taxi is often the only practical option. Follow signs for 'Official Taxis' and book with one of the marshalls. The official taxis should cost about USD 20, but you will still need to negotiate well to get that price. As in most places, it is best to ignore the many men offering taxis as soon as you walk out of the terminal.

Around the city

As explained in the detailed walking tours in this guide, the majority of sights are accessible on foot. However, for when feet get tired, or if the weather is not cooperating, the good news is that there are extensive public transport networks.

Tbilisi currently has a two-line **metro** system with a total of 22 stations. The longer red line has sixteen stops, and the green line has six. It runs from 6 am until midnight, and frequencies vary from every two-and-a-half minutes in the rush hour up to ten minutes off-peak. To use the metro system, you first need to buy a Metromoney card for 2 GED, which you can top up with whatever amount you choose. Each one-way ride costs 0.50 Tetri, regardless of length, making this one of the cheapest metro systems in the world. Signs and announcements are in Georgian and English, so it is easy to get around.

Baku's **bus** network spreads its tentacles across the entire city and out into the suburbs. They can take you just about anywhere you want to go. You can either pay on board by inserting the correct coins into a machine or use the Metromoney card. Buses are blue and yellow and display the route number on the front, and most bus stops have screens showing when the next bus is due. For full information in English on buses, including an interactive route planner and timetables, visit the Tbilisi Transport Company website.

Finally, you will see taxis cruising everywhere around Tbilisi, and you can easily hail one from the street. Mostly they are private taxis without a meter, so it is advisable to negotiate the fare before getting in. If you don't speak Georgian or Russia, it would be a good idea to have your destination written down or marked on a map to show the driver. While Uber does not yet operate in the city, a good alternative is the Taxify app.

— Where to stay —

Accommodation in Tbilisi often takes the form of small hotels, apartments and homestays. In recent years, more upmarket boutique style hotels have appeared, along with some of the bigger Western chains. If you are travelling during the peak summer months, you should try to book as far ahead as possible as there can be limited availability during that time. Here are just a few highlights in the top end and mid-range categories, although www.booking.com lists all the possible options at the competitive rates. Furthermore, Tripadvisor.com compares prices with the three or four top hotel consolidators, making sure you get the most reasonable rate. There is also a wide selection of apartments and rooms to rent in Tbilisi on www.airbnb.com.

Top end

Rooms Hotel is a top pick for Tbilisi. Housed in a converted industrial-style building, the beautifully designed hotel has a retro-Soviet style. The location is a bit out of the way, but a nice twenty to thirty minute stroll down Rustaveli Avenue sees you at Tbilisi old town.

Tbilisi Marriott is located right on Rustaveli Avenue near

Freedom Square. Classic luxury hotel in a historic building, with all you'd expect including an atrium-style lobby, twinkling crystal chandeliers, marble bathrooms and luxury bedrooms and a range of bars and restaurants.

Radisson Blu Iveria is on the upper part of Rustaveli Avenue, a few steps away from the metro station. This glass-fronted tower has an outdoor swimming pool, and all rooms have great views of either the Mtkvari river or Mtatsminda hill.

Courtyard Marriott directly faces onto Freedom Square, so you can't be more central than that. It has a heated indoor swimming pool and fitness centre.

Holiday Inn Tbilisi is a bit further out past Vera Park but is next to the Technical University metro station. The hotel is housed in a modern block, with an outdoor pool, and is handy for walks along the Mtkvari river.

Mid-Range

Ibis Styles Tbilisi Center is the cream of the crop in this category. Just 150 m south of Freedom Square, this newly-opened hotel is right in the heart of the old city. The hotel has a striking and colourful design throughout, and the highlight is the rooftop open-air bar and restaurant with panoramic views over Tbilisi. Ranked number one on Tripadvisor.

Mercure Tbilisi is a short walk from Gorgasali Square, Shardeni Street and Abanotubani. This modern four-star hotel comes with spa and sauna, and also boasts a rooftop bar.

Old Tiflis Boutique Hotel is in the Abanotubani area, with

Narikala Fortress a mere five-minute walk away. One of the neighbourhood's historic buildings houses this small and characterful hotel.

Shota Rustaveli Boutique Hotel is in a side street off Rustaveli Avenue next to the Georgian Parliament. The interior decor of the public areas and rooms is based on a twelfth-century poem written by Rustaveli himself. A stylish and unique place to stay.

YEREVAN | *Armenia*

Yerevan is a city full of contradictions and never fails to surprise first-time visitors. Laying claim to be one of the longest-inhabited cities in the world, few traces remain today of its history spanning three millennia. Wave after wave of conquering armies ensured that there was little left in their wake, and what remained was effectively erased by overzealous Soviet town planners.

Yerevan is a city of two halves. As you ride through the suburbs from the airport, you may find yourself wondering exactly where you have decided to visit. These outlying areas are characterised by abandoned, dilapidated factories and brutalist, crumbling Soviet-era apartment blocks. But once you get into the centre, Yerevan is a joy to be in; tree-lined boulevards, fountain-filled parks and squares and numerous open-air bistros and cafes lend the city a chic European air. Many prominent buildings are constructed from pink volcanic tuff, leading Pablo Neruda, Chilean Nobel-prize winning novelist, to describe the city as 'harmonic like a rose, one of the most beautiful cities in the world.'

In the surrounding Armenian countryside, astounding historical sites litter the landscape. From the UNESCO World Heritage Sites of Vagharshapat through to ancient monasteries and Greco-Roman temples, there are plenty to keep even the most intrepid explorers busy for many days.

A towering backdrop to all of this is the majestic Mount Ararat, where Noah's Ark supposedly came to rest after the biblical flood. This striking feature is bound to feature heavily in the many photos you will take during your stay.

There has never been a better time to visit Yerevan. The city offers a modern, traveller-friendly infrastructure, with a wide selection of hotels and restaurants catering to every taste. Many of the sights are clustered conveniently in the centre, enabling leisurely walking tours. And the visa regime is now relatively relaxed, with many nationalities eligible to apply for e-visas. This book will be your companion as you explore the city. Welcome to Yerevan.

Contents

* * *

List of Maps

Getting to know Yerevan

A Brief History

Yerevan claims to be one of the oldest continually-inhabited cities, and as we can trace its history to at least the eighth century BC, this seems to be a valid claim indeed. Back then, in 782 BC, Argishti I, King of Urartu, a territory roughly corresponding to that of Armenia today, established the fortress of Erebuni, on the site of today's Yerevan. While he intended to create a 'great administrative and religious centre and a fully royal capital', the prime function of the fort was to act as a defence against attacks from further afield.

Alas, the fortress did little to keep back the waves of invasions, and the settlement witnessed a rapid procession of new rulers as the centuries rolled by. The original Kingdom of Urartu fell in 590 BC, coming under the control of the Median Empire, which forty years later was subsumed by Cyrus the Great into the mighty Persian Achaemenid Empire. This shift in power ushered in a couple of centuries of relative stability. Erebuni became a major economic centre of the subsequent Satrapy of Armenia and steadily changed into a city characterised by a robust Persian culture.

However, the rise of Alexander the Great threatened this peace and prosperity. Eventually, he invaded the Achaemenid Empire, and following the decisive victory of Alexander's forces over the Persians at the Battle of Gaugamala in 331 BC, the rulers of the Satrapy of Armenia successfully won independence to form the Kingdom of Armenia. They viewed Erebuni as a product of Persian heritage, and so subsequent kings built new commercial centres in places such as Vagharshapat and Dvin.

Erebuni accordingly lost its role as a strategic centre, and slowly faded into obscurity over the following centuries. Little is known from this period, although in 301 AD it was recorded that King Tiridates III declared Armenia a Christian country. Throughout the fourth and fifth centuries, Armenia fell under the control of the Persians again, this time the Sasanian Empire. Yerevan remained as something of a backwater during their tenure, as it did so throughout the subsequent Arab invasion and two centuries of Islamic rule. The next centuries saw the waves of invaders continue; Yerevan witnessed the rule of Byzantines, Seljuks, Mongols and Turkic tribes. It was not until 1441, when the seat of the Armenian church was moved back to Vagharshapat, that Yerevan slowly regained its crown of economic, cultural, religious and administrative centre.

In 1501, Armenia was absorbed into the powerful Persian Safavid Empire, and it remained under Persian influence, with some brief intermissions, right up until the beginning of the nineteenth century. Yerevan became capital of the Persian administrative territory of Erivan Beglarbegi and accordingly grew in importance. In 1828, after the Russo-Persian War, Yerevan, along with the rest of eastern Armenia, was ceded by the Persians to the Russians. It became part of the Russian empire and capital of the Erivan Governate. The Russians actively promoted the resettlement of ethnic Armenians from

Persia and Turkey, and so the population rocketed. In the latter part of the nineteenth century, development took off, with many new schools, factories and other facilities built, and much new infrastructure put in place.

When the Russian Empire fell as a result of the 1917 revolution, the newly-independent Republic of Armenia was founded, with Yerevan as its capital. However, after a few short years, the nation fell to the Bolsheviks, and the Soviet Union took full control of the country in 1920. Under Soviet rule, a comprehensive urban plan, designed by the Armenian architect Alexander Tamanian, was implemented with the aim of growing the city to 150,000. In reality, it developed to such an extent that Yerevan was transformed into a modern industrial city of about one million.

Once the Soviet Union collapsed in 1991, Yerevan became the capital of the newly-independent Republic of Armenia. After 2000, a new surge in development took place, which continues to this day.

Geography

Yerevan is Armenia's capital, situated in the centre-west of the country, only 15 km from the border with Turkey. The city is around one thousand metres above sea level on the Ararat plain and spreads out either side of the Hrazdan river. The city is bounded to the north by mountain ranges, which include the lofty Mount Aragats, while to the south the magnificent Mount Ararat forms an impressive backdrop to the city.

There are twelve administrative districts, yet most tourist sights of Yerevan are concentrated in the Kentron district, easily distinguishable on maps as a circle, bounded on its eastern edge by parkland. Right at its heart is Republic

Square, a focal point for most visitors.

Demographics

Just over one million people live in Yerevan, which means that around a third of the entire Armenian people live within city limits. In line with the nation as a whole, the population of Yerevan is decreasing. This decline is due to a mix of factors but primarily results from high emigration rates, which have seen 1.5 million Armenians move abroad since independence in 1991. Lower family sizes, resulting from economic conditions and changing social norms, exacerbates this situation.

While Yerevan today is overwhelmingly Armenian, this wasn't always the case, and there used to be notable minority populations of Azerbaijanis and Russians. All of the former have now left, particularly after the Nagorno-Karabakh war, and many of the Russians went back to their homeland during the 1990s economic crisis.

The majority of people (93%) follow Armenian Apostolic Christianity. Although the religion suffered oppression during the Soviet era, it is once again flourishing, and the city is home to the Saint Gregory the Illuminator Cathedral, the largest Armenian church in the world. There is tolerance for all religions in the country, and Yerevan is also home to a Russian Orthodox church and the Shia Blue Mosque. Other small minorities include Jews and Yezidis.

Languages

Armenian is the official language, an independent branch of

the Indo-European linguistic group, spoken by 98% of citizens. It has its own alphabet, devised in the fifth century by Mesrop Mashtots. The most widely-spoken second language is Russian.

Yerevan Walking Tour 1 - Navigating north of Republic Square

This walking tour begins in the very heart of Yerevan, Republic Square. It takes in all the sights to the north of the square in a route which should require a full day. But don't worry, along the way there are many leafy parks to take a breather, and welcoming cafes to take refreshments and rest your weary feet.

* * *

Map A: Republic Square to Northern Avenue

Key:
1. *Republic Square*
2. *History Museum of Armenia*
3. *Arno Babajanyan Concert Hall*
4. *Northern Avenue*

Republic Square

Republic Square *(Map A, Point 1)* is the starting point of this walking tour. Standing in front of the dancing fountains, the grand facade of the History Museum of Armenia will be directly in front of you. Turn to the right, and you will see Government House with its distinctive clock tower, and then at the five o'clock position the grand arches of the Trade Unions and Communications building. Turn to the left, and there is Government House number two, and then the Armenia Marriott Hotel at the eight o'clock position.

It is immediately apparent that the same architect designed these buildings, all built from pink and yellow tuff stone in the neoclassical style. The man responsible was Alexander Tamanian, whose work you will often encounter during any wanderings around Yerevan. He designed the layout of the square and its buildings in 1924, and by the 1950s the ensemble was completed. This was during Soviet times, and so the square was named Lenin Square after the great revolutionary leader. It was not until after independence that it became known as Republic Square. Leading world architects have duly lauded this space as one of the finest centrally-planned squares around.

Today, the square is a favourite meeting place for locals and visitors alike. At night in the summer it comes to life, with the undoubted highlight being the 'Dancing Fountains' in front of the museum. As its name suggests, the water is choreographed perfectly to a variety of tunes, from Armenian patriotic songs and Russian classical music through to modern-day pop hits. The unmissable show starts at 9 pm and lasts for two hours.

History Museum of Armenia

Since its foundation in 1919, the History Museum of Armenia (*Map A, Point 2*) has acted as the de facto national museum, supported and funded by the Armenian government. It is a great place to begin any trip to Armenia, as it presents a comprehensive overview of the complicated history of the country, from the Palaeolithic period one million years ago right up to the present day.

The museum has four collections. The archaeological department shows objects dating up until the fifteenth century. An ethnographic section displays seventeenth to twentieth-century cultural artefacts from all regions of Armenia, including carpets, wood carvings, copperwork, clothing and other decorative-applied art. The numismatic collection displays coins found in Armenia dating from Greek and Roman times through to the present day, and documentary department exhibits photographic evidence of Armenian monuments that have today either vanished or destroyed.

The museum is open daily from 11 am to 6 pm, except on Mondays and national holidays when it remains closed. The entrance fee is 2000 AMD and tickets can be bought online at https://historymuseum.am/en. Foreign language guided tours are available for 5000 AMD.

As you face the History Museum from Republic Square, walk up Abovyan Street that runs to the left of the building.

Arno Babajanyan Concert Hall

The first rather austere-looking grey building, with brown window frames, is the Arno Babajanyan Concert Hall *(Map A, Point 3)*. Founded in 1921, this entertainment venue takes its name from the esteemed Armenian composer. Babajanyan, a native of Yerevan, was something of a child musical prodigy, and from the age of seven studied at the Yerevan State Musical Conservatory. After a stint in Russia, he moved back to Yerevan and taught at his old music school from 1950-56.

During this time he wrote his masterpiece Piano Trio in F sharp minor. He also collaborated with national poets, and much of his musical works are rooted in Armenian folklore.

Continue along Abovyan Street for around 50 m. Turn left along Northern Avenue, which stretches off at an angle towards the opera house.

Northern Avenue

This broad pedestrianised street *(Map A, Point 4)* links Abovyan Street to the Armenian Opera Theatre and is a relatively recent addition to the city plan, built only in 2007. High-end apartment buildings line the street, along with hotels, restaurants and luxury shops offering a bewildering array of world-famous brands. You will often see both residents and visitors promenading here on summer evenings.

The avenue was initially designed by celebrated Armenian architect Alexander Tamanian, who formulated the city centre layout plan for Yerevan in 1924 and created Republic Square and the Opera Theatre. However, his vision for this grand avenue did not become a reality until the city council decided to revive his plans. By this time, many existing buildings laid in the path of the planned thoroughfare, so the local authorities had to embark upon a controversial programme of buying out the landowners and consolidating all the various plots of land.

Today, eleven nine-storey buildings line the street, clad in a variety of basalt, granite and limestones. You will see escalators going underground at various points, and these lead to a parking area and subterranean mall.

Northern Avenue is just under half a kilometre long and

ends near Freedom Square.

At the end of Northern Avenue, cross Tumanyan Street. Go straight and walk towards Freedom Square.

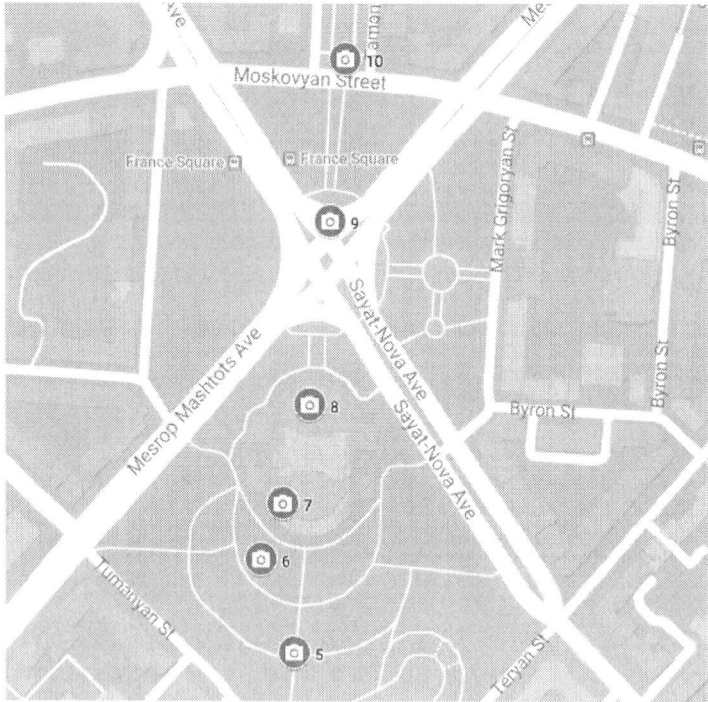

Map B: Freedom Square to Cafesjian Sculpture Gallery

Key:
   5. Freedom Square
   6. Statue of Alexander Spendiaryan
   7. Armenia Opera Theatre
   8. Aram Khatchaturian Concert Hall
   9. France Square
   10. Cafesjian Sculpture Gallery

Capitals of the Caucasus

* * *

Freedom Square

The expanse of Freedom Square *(Map B, Point 5)* and the grand facade of the Armenia Opera Theatre will be directly in front of you. Surrounding the square is the Opera Park, which takes up an entire city block. Here, particularly on the left side, there is a procession of pavement cafes and restaurants, and in the summer is a relaxing and peaceful place to have drinks and snacks. To the right is the Swan Lake, replete with paddle boats to hire.

Freedom Square itself is somewhat misleadingly named, as its expanse of concrete actually forms a gigantic circle. Regardless of its nomenclature, the square has played a crucial role in the political life of Armenia. Time and again it has acted as the focal point for demonstrations, as the sheer scale of the space allows gatherings of more than 50,000 people. In 1988, the Karabakh movement, which advocated the seizure of Armenian-dominated Nagorno-Karabakh from Azerbaijan, held mass rallies here. After independence, protests have occurred after most national elections.

Statue of Alexander Spendiaryan

In the centre of the square on a monumental plinth is a statue of Alexander Spendiaryan *(Map B, Point 6)*, a renowned composer and conductor, born in Russia in 1871 to Armenian parents. He went on to compose acclaimed operas, symphonies and choral works, and to lead concerts all over Russia.

In his early years, he took private composition lessons from

129

the legendary Rimsky-Korsakov, who regarded Spendniaryan as something of a protegee. His teacher's opinion turned out to be entirely correct. In 1924, he arrived in Yerevan and conducted a small orchestra comprising the students and teachers from the local conservatory. It became clear to Spendiaryan that there was the potential in Armenia to support a fully-fledged symphony orchestra, and he duly formed this the next year. It eventually became the Armenian State Orchestra. During this time, he also composed the 'Yerevan Sketches', widely-acclaimed experimental compositions that made use of ancient Armenian instruments. Spendiaryan died shortly after that in 1928 and is buried nearby in the grounds of the Opera Theatre, which was subsequently named after him.

Armenia Opera Theatre

This grand edifice *(Map B, Point 7)* was designed by Alexander Tamanian, the same architect responsible for the layout of the city centre and Republic Square, and opened to great fanfare in 1933, at a time when Armenian was experiencing severe economic problems, and the people were living through considerable hardship. The building of this opera house acted as a beacon, showing that there is a higher purpose in life, despite temporary financial difficulties. From its very first day, the Opera Theatre has been the cultural heart of Yerevan and the entire country. Its main auditorium seats an audience of 1050.

There had been a rich history of opera in Armenia since the mid-nineteenth century, with the most important operas referred to as the 'three As': *Anush*, *Almast* and *Arshak II*. Yet there was a lack of a suitable venue; the Opera Theatre filled this gap, prompted a renewed interest in the art form, and resulted in many new compositions and the discovery of promising talents. Soon after the establishment of the Opera Theatre, a ballet troupe was formed, with the inaugural performance of Swan Lake in 1935. A few years later, the first Armenian ballet written by Aram Khachaturian, *Happiness*, debuted here, the success of which led him to write his masterpiece, *Gayane*, which has garnered international critical acclaim. Together, the Opera Theatre has staged more than two hundred different operas and ballets, and overseas tours have reached twenty countries.

Walk around to the other side of the building, where you will find the Aram Khatchaturian Concert Hall.

Aram Khatchaturian Concert Hall

Complementing the Opera Theatre is the grandiose Aram Khatchaturian Concert Hall *(Map B, Point 8)*, also designed and built by Tamanian. This is home to the Armenian Philharmonic Orchestra, founded in 1924, whose musicians are picked from the very best talent at the Yerevan Conservatory and leading music schools in Moscow and St. Petersburg. Its main auditorium can seat 1300 people.

The concert hall is named after Aram Khatchaturian, the esteemed Armenian composer and conductor. In much of his compositions, he incorporated Armenian folk music traditions, and his works are still enjoyed today and performed regularly. It is safe to say that he has 'national treasure' status, and the government has honoured him on postage stamps and banknotes. A statue of the great man is in pride of place directly outside the concert hall's main entrance.

* * *

France Square

The concert hall faces out on to one of Yerevan's busiest intersections, France Square *(Map B, Point 9)*. Stranded in the very centre of this melee of traffic is a bronze statue of the French painter Jules Bastien-Lepage. Remarkably, this sculpture is by Auguste Rodin, probably one of the most sought-after sculptors of the nineteenth and twentieth centuries. France gave the sculpture as a gift in 2011 to mark the twentieth anniversary of Armenian independence and it was unveiled by then-president Nikola Sarkozy.

The two countries continue to have a close relationship, as France was one of the only places to provide a haven for Armenian refugees fleeing the 1915 genocide. France has also officially recognised the events of that year as genocide and continues to press Turkey to do the same, earning much gratitude from Armenians.

Cross over to the far side of France Square and continue straight. The Yerevan Cascade is directly ahead, fronted by the Cafesjian Sculpture Gallery.

Cafesjian Sculpture Gallery

The formal garden area *(Map B, Point 10)* in front of the Yerevan Cascade is the perfect space for the display of an intriguing collection of contemporary sculpture. The park's long uncluttered walkways and formal stretches of lawn ensure that the artworks stand out and that people can fully appreciate them from all angles.

As you enter the garden, you first encounter a striking statue of Alexander Tamanian, the architect whose designs had such a profound impact on Yerevan's cityscape. As we have seen, he was responsible for the overall city plan of wide boulevards, parks, squares and the Opera Theatre, and rightly deserves to have his statue in such a prominent place. It shows Tamanian hunched over a drawing board, pondering his work at hand, and perhaps captures a moment when he was creating the blueprint of the city we are walking around today.

You can get up close and personal with the sculptures of many leading modern artists from around the world. Three of the most striking are the 'Woman Smoking', 'Roman Warrior' and 'Cat' sculpted by Colombian artist Fernando Botero. His signature style is the depiction of people and animals with a large, exaggerated volume.   This style has become so recognisable it has given birth to the artistic genre 'Boterismo'. Yerevan is indeed lucky to host these three statues, and his other similarly-proportioned works can be found in prestigious locations around the world from Fifth Avenue in New York to the Champs Elysees in Paris. Another series of sculptures in the garden are the dynamic hares of Britsh artist Barry Flanagan, in a variety of acrobatic poses.

When walking up through the garden also look out for a jolly giant blue kiwi from American artist Peter Woytuk. He specialises in such enchanting sculptures of birds and animals, and he has designed a whole menagerie of chickens, ravens, sheep, cats and more, which are in prominent public places throughout America.

There is a whole host of noteworthy sculptures to enjoy around this space, including rearing horses made from horseshoes, a beautiful composition of leaping gazelles, an open latticework giant teapot, and a thinking man composed entirely of letters of the alphabet. Its a thought-provoking place to spend some time, and if you enjoyed it, there are yet more examples of modern sculpture placed along the various levels of the Yerevan Cascade.

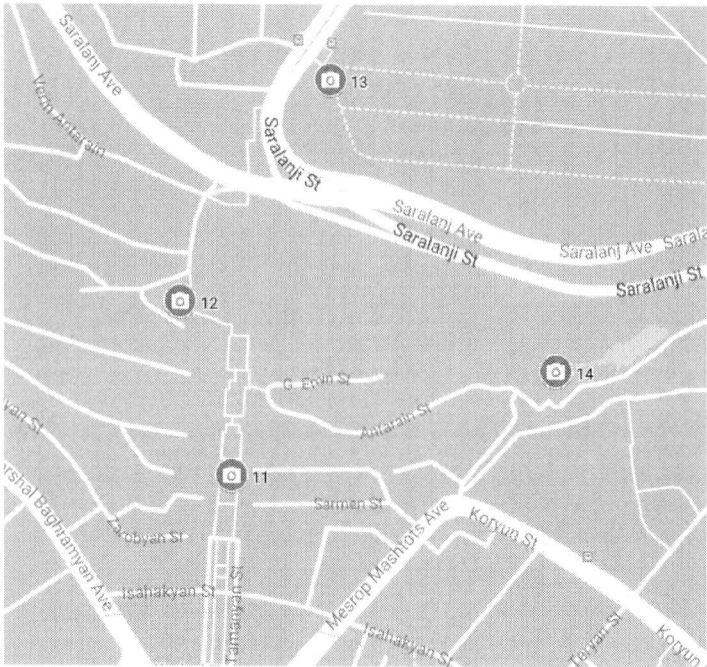

Map C: Yerevan Cascade to Matenadaran

Key:
11. *Yerevan Cascade*
12. *Charles Aznavour House Museum*
13. *Victory Park*
14. *Matenadaran*

Yerevan Cascade

From the Cafesjian Sculpture Gallery, cross Isahakyan Street to begin your ascent of this mighty limestone staircase *(Map*

C, Point 11). This was designed by prominent Armenian architects to link the central areas of Yerevan city with the Monument district higher up the hillside and has around five hundred steps.

The views from the top are nothing short of spectacular, and you will see the whole city spread in front of you, with the mighty Mount Ararat as a snow-capped backdrop. It can be hard work climbing up this flight of stairs, particularly if you have a rather sedentary lifestyle, but for those of us keen to save our legs there is good news. Just enter one of the entry doors at each level, and you will find much-needed escalators waiting to whisk you to the top.

At the top of the Yerevan Cascade, take the path that exits to the left. The Charles Aznavour House Museum will be directly in front of you.

Charles Aznavour House Museum

This museum *(Map C, Point 12)* honours the life and works of the French-Armenian singer, songwriter and actor Charles Aznavour. Established in 2011, Aznavour himself cut the ribbon at the inauguration ceremony, while the Armenian President Serzh Sargsyan and French President Nicolas Sarkozy looked on. In the words of the Armenian president at the event, Charles Aznavour 'is truly a legend, a legend that belongs not only to France and Armenia but also the humanity at large'.

Aznavour was born in Paris in 1924, the son of Armenian immigrants who fled to France from the instability at that time. He was discovered by the singer Edith Piaf, who then took him on tour around the US and France. He quickly gained immense popularity, and went on to write more than a thousand songs and record a hundred records. In 1998, CNN viewers voted him the Entertainer of the Century, head of such worthies as Elvis and Bob Dylan. Throughout his decades-long career, he sang for presidents, popes and royalty.

The five storey building comprises the personal apartment of Aznavour, studios, workshop spaces, an open-air concert venue, and the museum itself which displays various artefacts such as albums, books, photographs, awards and portraits. The building is modern in style, with minimalistic, clean lines. Its location high above Yerevan at the top of the Cascade ensures panoramic view, and the architect Narek Sargsyan included a 'spatial gate', a portal which frames a spectacular view of the city and Mount Ararat in the distance.

From the museum, walk uphill along the small street. At the end, turn right, and under the overhanging concrete platform take the stairs up. After admiring the view from this open space, walk past the big obelisk, and the entrance to Victory Park will be 50 m ahead on your right.

Victory Park

Victory Park *(Map C, Point 13)* is a vast green space on the uplands of Yerevan, just above the Cascades complex. It marks the victory of the USSR in World War II. The main reason to visit this park, other than the fantastic views, is to see the Mother Armenia statue, which is visible from just about the entire city.

The statue, built from copper, is 22 metres high, and with the basalt pedestal the entire monument is more than 50 metres in stature. Mother Armenia symbolises peace through strength, and with her sword in hand is widely-regarded as a guardian of Yerevan and the whole country. Inside the base of the statue is a museum detailing the bloody Armenian participation in World War II, where more than 300,000 nationals died, with further exhibits on the 1988-1994 Nagorno-Karabakh war with Azerbaijan.

Next to the statue is the Grave of the Unknown Soldier, commemorating all those who lost their lives defending Armenia. On 9 May each year these two sites are the focus of the nation's commemorations of the fallen, and on that day politicians lay wreaths and thousands of Armenians visit to pay their respects.

From the park, you can either retrace your steps back to the top of the Cascade and then walk down to street level, or to save your weary feet, jump in a taxi and proceed directly to the Matenadaran.

Matenadaran

The Mesrop Mashtots Institute of Ancient Manuscripts (*Map C, Point 14*), otherwise known as Matenadaran is one of the absolute highlights of any visit to Yerevan. It is a treasure trove of ancient knowledge and is undoubtedly one of the world's greatest stores of medieval books and manuscripts, which cover a wide range of subjects from theology and history through to medicine and astronomy. In recognition of its importance, UNESCO has inscribed the Matenadaran on its 'Memory of the World' programme.

The term matenadaran in Armenian means 'repository of manuscripts'. There has been a long history of such stores of ancient books and documents in the country, and as far back as the fifth century, local historians have recorded the existence of a matenadaran at the Etchmiadzin cathedral. However, due to Armenia's particularly turbulent history, with successive waves of hostile invaders over the centuries, many manuscripts were lost through looting. It was only after the country's absorption into the Russian Empire that the collection stabilised. In World War I, the authorities moved all the artefacts to Moscow for safekeeping, which turned out to be unfortunate timing with the Bolsheviks seizing the entire collection during the revolution. It was only after another four years that the treasures were returned. In the years after, the whole matenadaran became state property, and the order was given to construct the museum, subsequently completed in 1957.

The building, designed by Armenia architect Mark Grigoryan, has a dominating position on top of a small hill overlooking Yerevan. It is made from basalt and incorporates key Armenian architectural traits. It is fronted by two terraces; on the upper level are a series of statues depicting renowned Armenian scholars, while on the lower level is a much bigger monument to Meshrop Mashtots, the creator of the Armenian alphabet, and his student Korian.

The core of the collection comprises 23,000 handwritten and illustrated books and manuscripts. Many books have stunning leather covers with a variety of stamped and embossed designs. Inside are many beautiful examples of miniature paintings and the most exquisite calligraphy. You will see many texts in Armenia, but also many in Persian, Arabic and other languages. Any bibliophile will be in heaven.

The museum is open daily from 10 am to 5 pm, except on Sundays, Mondays and public holidays when it remains closed. Guided tours are available in nine languages.

From Matenadarn, walk back downhill along Mesrop Mashtots Avenue. Just before you get back to France Square, turn right on Moskovyan Street, and the entrance to the Yervand Kochar

Museum will be on your left.

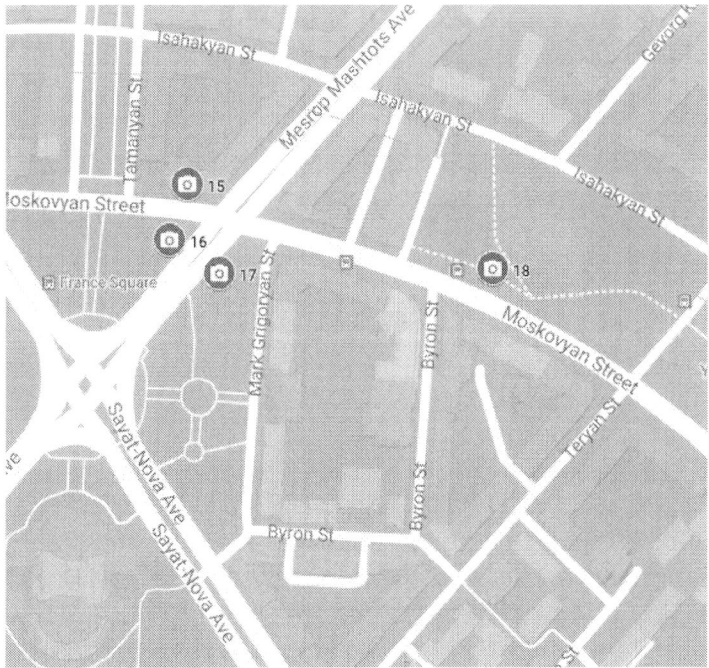

Map D: Yervand Kochar Museum to Poplavok Park

Key:
15. *Yervand Kochar Museum*
16. *William Saroyan Statue*
17. *Sayat-Nova Monument*
18. *Poplavok Park and Holocaust Memorial*

Yervand Kochar Museum

Yervand Kochar was the founder of the fascinating *Peinture dans L'espace*, or Painting in Space, school of twentieth-century modern art, and this museum *(Map D, Point 15)* is on the site of the renowned artist's former studio.

Kochar's revolutionary artistic movement freed traditional painting from the constraints of two-dimensional canvases and blended it with sculpture to create a three-dimensional artwork. Painting in Space comprises differently-shaped metal panels covered with various paintings. A small engine in the pedestal of the artwork rotates the whole structure, so introducing the dynamic concepts of motion and time into the piece of art.

Kochar was born in 1899 in Tbilisi, Georgia, to Armenia parents. He spent much of his early life there, with a brief break during which he moved to Moscow to study Fine Arts. Upon finishing his education in 1919, he returned to Tbilisi to work as a high school painting teacher, a shortlived career which ended when he moved abroad in 1922. He eventually made it to Paris, where his career took off. It was here that he forged the Painting in Space movement, and participated in many notable exhibitions alongside other Avant-Garde artists such as Picasso, Matisse and Chagall.

In 1936, Kochar took everyone by surprise by relocating to Moscow, which turned out to be a monumental mistake. The Soviets accused him of anti-state propaganda and anti-revolutionary activities, and eventually imprisoned him from 1941 to 1943. Upon his release, Kochar returned to his homeland of Armenia, where he embarked upon another three productive decades which saw many new masterpieces. His best-known work from this period is the statue of David of Sassoun, currently outside Yerevan railway station, and the epic 'Disasters of War' painting.

The museum brings together many examples of artistic output from the artist's Tbilisi, Paris and Yerevan periods, and you can view a wide array of paintings and sculptures. And this museum is the only place, other than the Pompidou

Capitals of the Caucasus

Centre in Paris, where you can enjoy seeing 'Painting in Space'.

Entry costs 500 AMD, and a highly recommended guided tour is available from 2000 AMD. It is open from 11 am to 5 pm every day except Mondays.

From the main entrance of Yervand Kochar Museum, cross Moskovyan Street. Directly in front of you on the corner is a statue of William Saroyan.

William Saroyan statue

This statue *(Map D, Point 16)* depicts William Saroyan, a Pulitzer Prize-winning Armenian-American novelist and playwright, born to Armenian immigrant parents in California in 1908. He grew up among an impoverished community of other exiled Armenian children, an early life which provided much raw material for his later works.

Saroyan's career as a writer had its root in the Great American Depression, with a series of stories which celebrated the joys of life despite severe hardships and hunger. Much of his creative output was semi-autobiographical, feeding on his childhood and family experiences. He received much critical acclaim in the 1940s, first for his much-celebrated play *The Time of Your Life*. Soon after that success, he wrote the film script for The Human Comedy. While the movie, starring Mickey Rooney, was a success, Saroyan was unhappy with it, and instead turned it into a bestselling novel.

From 1958 onwards, Saroyan spent most of his time in Europe, and Paris in particular. The piling up of debts, accrued from his insatiable travelling, gambling and drinking, drove his writing, and he once said that to write for him was 'simply to stay alive in an interesting way.' Saroyan died in 1981, and while he rests at peace California, his heart is buried at Yerevan's Pantheon Park.

Cross over the busy Mesrop Mashtots Avenue.

Sayat-Nova Monument

Facing William Saroyan's statue across Mesrop Mashtots Avenue is the monument to the eighteenth-century Armenian poet and folk-songwriter Sayat-Nova *(Map D, Point 17)*. He composed more than 220 songs and in Armenian, Georgian, Azerbaijani and Persian. Armenians regard him as one of their most celebrated poets, and to honour his legacy this memorial was erected in 1963 to mark the 250th anniversary of his birth. A major thoroughfare just around the corner was also named after the great bard, as was the music school directly behind the monument.

At the height of his fame, Sayat-Nova performed at the court of Georgian King Erekle II. His linguistic ability lead to him to become a diplomat, and the poet was responsible for negotiating alliances between Armenia, Georgia and Persia. However, he let romance get the better of him when he fell in love with the King's sister Ana. He was thrown out in disgrace and found work as a wandering musician. Eventually, he became an Armenian Apostolic priest.

His story comes to an abrupt end in 1795 during the Persian invasion at the Haghpat Monastery in the north of Armenia. The Shah of Iran, Agha Mohammad Khan, demanded that Sayat-Nova convert to Islam. When he vehemently refused, he was summarily beheaded. He rests today at the Cathedral of St. George in Tbilisi.

* * *

Walk a few steps back to the junction with Moskovyan Street, and turn right. Continue for 100 m to Poplavok Park.

Poplavok Park and Holocaust Memorial

Poplavok Park *(Map D, Point 18)* is the beginning of the much larger Circular Park, which arcs around the eastern half of the city centre as far as Saint Gregory the Illuminator Cathedral. Poplavok means 'fishing float' in Russian, and the park was named as such as it appears to be bobbing on the water of its central lake. Overlooking the lake is a restaurant complex, and in the summer it is a relaxing place to have a bite to eat while watching the fountains.

Tucked away in the southeastern corner of the park, near the junction of Moskovyan Street and Teryan Street, is the Holocaust Memorial. This aims to show the solidarity that exists between Armenians and Jews, both of whom endured cataclysmic genocides in the early twentieth century. The Armenian genocide occurred in 1915 at the hands of the Ottoman Turks, who endeavoured to exterminate the population altogether. Just a few years later Hitler attempted to do the same to the Jews, and because of their previous experience, many Armenians helped Jews to escape at that time.

The inscription reads: 'To live and never forget: In memory of the victims of both the Armenian Genocide and Jewish Holocaust.

From the Holocaust Memorial, turn left up Teryan Street. Turn right along Isahakyan Street and go one block to the junction with Abovyan Street, where you should turn left. Then look for a side road on your left. The Derinik Demirchyan House Museum is in apartment building 29.

***

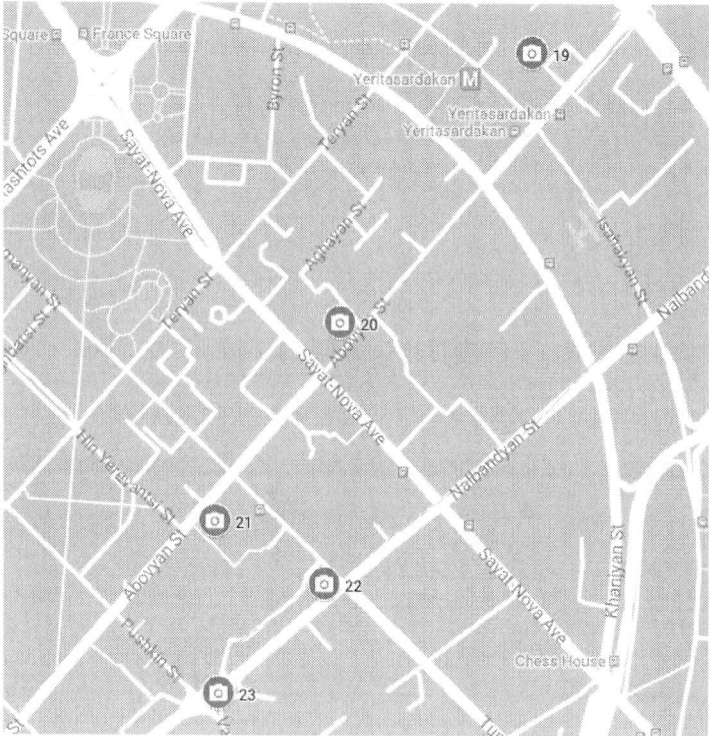

Map E: Derenik Demirchyan House Museum to Sakharov
Square

Key:
  19. Derenik Demirchyan House Museum
  20. Abovyan Street and Holy Mother of God Kathoghike Church
  21. Charles Aznavour Square
  22. House Museum of Alexander Spendiaryan
  23. Sakharov Square

Derenik Demirchyan House Museum

This nondescript apartment building *(Map E, Point 19)* on Aboyvan Street was home to the famous Armenian writer, poet, playwright and translator, Derenik Demirchyan. He lived here from 1929 until he died in 1956, and his home is now a memorial and museum.

During his childhood, Demirchyan attended school in Tbilisi. He then returned to Yerevan where he became a part of the *Vernatun* intellectual literary group established by the national poet Tumanyan. He soon published his first set of poetry in 1899. In the 1920s, many of his plays came to notice and were staged across the Caucasus, including his best-known work *Nazar the Brave* which was eventually made into a film. Demirchyan then branched out into writing, with his magnum opus being the epic 1940s patriotic book *Vardanank*. He also translated great Russian novels into Armenian. The museum comprises three memorial rooms and a large exhibition hall. There are hundreds of artefacts on display that illustrate the writer's productive life, including a remarkable Stradivarius violin.

The museum entrance fee is 300 AMD, and it is open every day from 11 am to 5 pm, except for Mondays when it remains closed. Entrance is free on the last Saturday of every month.

Once you conclude your visit to the museum, retrace your steps back down Abovyan Street to the junction with Isahakyan Street. At that point, continue straight.

Abovyan Street and Holy Mother of God Kathoghike Church

Abovyan Street is one of the most prominent thoroughfares in the centre of Yerevan, running southwest in a straight line from Khachatur Abovyan Square to Republic Square. Along its length are many landmarks, ranging from governmental, cultural, educational and religious buildings, through to luxury hotels, restaurants, residential buildings and high-end retail. It's the Yerevan equivalent of Fifth Avenue in New York. It is a pleasant place to stroll, window shop and people watch, particularly in the summer months when the trees provide much-needed shade.

Walk straight for 300 metres, and on the corner of Abovyan Street and Sayat-Nova Avenue is a compound with two very different churches *(Map E, Point 20)*. The larger of the two is the Saint Anna Church, opened just recently in 2009. The much smaller Holy Mother of God Kathoghike Church in front of it dates back to the thirteenth century and is the oldest surviving Catholic church in Yerevan.

The medieval church was for centuries hidden from view. After the 1679 earthquake, a large basilica was erected on this site. It was not until the 1930s, when Soviet authorities began to demolish the basilica to make way for an apartment block, that the original thirteenth-century church was found encased within its walls. Archaeologists managed to persuade the Soviets to preserve the building.

Continue walking down Abovyan Street until Charles Aznavour Square.

Charles Aznavour Square

This small-scale and cosy square *(Map E, Point 21)*, named after the Armenian superstar, is buzzing with activity most of the day, particularly during the summer months. The square is bordered on one side by Abovyan Street.

In the northeastern corner is the imposing collonaded facade of the **Moscow Cinema**. This entertainment venue has four main halls and an open-air theatre and hosts the annual Golden Apricot International Film Festival. Before the construction of the cinema in 1936, this was the site of the Saint Paul and Peter Church, then one of the oldest in the city with parts dating back to the fifth and sixth centuries. However, the Soviet authorities demolished this in 1930 as part of a coordinated programme of religious vandalism which saw many similarly-ancient churches razed to the ground. Thankfully, some frescoes were salvaged from the ruins and are now on display in the Yerevan History Museum.

Recently, the Moscow Cinema has ironically been at the heart of a similar religious controversy. This time the government proposed building a new church on the site of the open-air theatre part of the cinema. This proposed construction prompted such outrage from the public that even the Prime Minister got involved, so they dropped the plans.

Dotted around the square are some of the **surreal sculptures** of Armenian artist, Ara Alekyan. These artworks occasionally change as the sculptor creates new pieces, but two long-standing residents of Charles Aznavour Square are the giant spider and bear sculptures. These are made entirely from scrap metal, such as bolts, pipes, girders and so on.

147

Alekyan was first inspired to create such artworks in the aftermath of the devastating 1988 earthquake, when he imagined sculptures coming out of the wreckage and subsequently used the ruined metal in his artwork. He now sources his materials from scrap metal dealers, and creates the pieces by first welding the metal into the desired shape and then setting the entire ensemble on fire to create a uniform burnished effect. If you are lucky, you might see Alekyan at one of his statues. He visits them every week to fix the cracks and other minor damage caused by children climbing all over them.

While in the square, also make sure to visit the unique **fountain**, surrounding which are statues of all twelve zodiac signs, each spurting water into the central pool.

Finally, to the south of the square is the 1920s neoclassical facade of the opulent Grand Hotel Yerevan, a great place to pop into for a reviving drink, lunch or afternoon tea,

Retrace your steps a few metres back up Abovyan Street and then turn right onto Tumanyan Street which runs behind the Moscow Cinema. After 100 m you will come across the House Museum of Alexander Spendiaryan, at the junction with Nalbandyan Street.

House Museum of Alexander Spendiaryan

Here at 21 Nalbandyan Street *(Map E, Point 22)*, we encounter Alexander Spendiaryan, the musical genius, composer and conductor again. He spent the last four years of his life living in an apartment within this block, which is now a memorial museum. The flat comprises three rooms, throughout which many personal artefacts are displayed such as photos, documents, handwritten notes and first editions of his compositions. There is also a reconstruction of his studio.

The museum is open daily from 11 am to 5 pm, except on Mondays when it stays closed.

From the museum continue south down Nalbandyan Street until you reach Sakharov Square.

Sakharov Square

In the centre of the busy intersection of Sakharov Square *(Map E, Point 23)* is a rather pensive-looking bust of the Russian nuclear physicist and disarmament advocate, Andrei Sakharov. The scientist designed Russia's first generation of thermonuclear weapons but later turned his attention to promoting peace and human rights, earning him state-sponsored persecution. In recognition of his activism, he won the Nobel Peace Prize in 1975. This statue in Yerevan is one of many that can be found across Russia and further afield around the world.

Continue along Nalbandyan Street south from Sakharov Square, and you will pass the Republic Square metro station. A further 100 m will see you back at Republic Square, which is the endpoint of this walking tour.

Yerevan Walking Tour 2 - Stepping south of Republic Square

This walking tour begins at Republic Square. Walk up Nalbandyan Street, which runs to the right of the History Museum of Armenia and the Dancing Fountains. After 50 metres or so you will see the Republic Square Metro Station, at which point you should turn right.

* * *

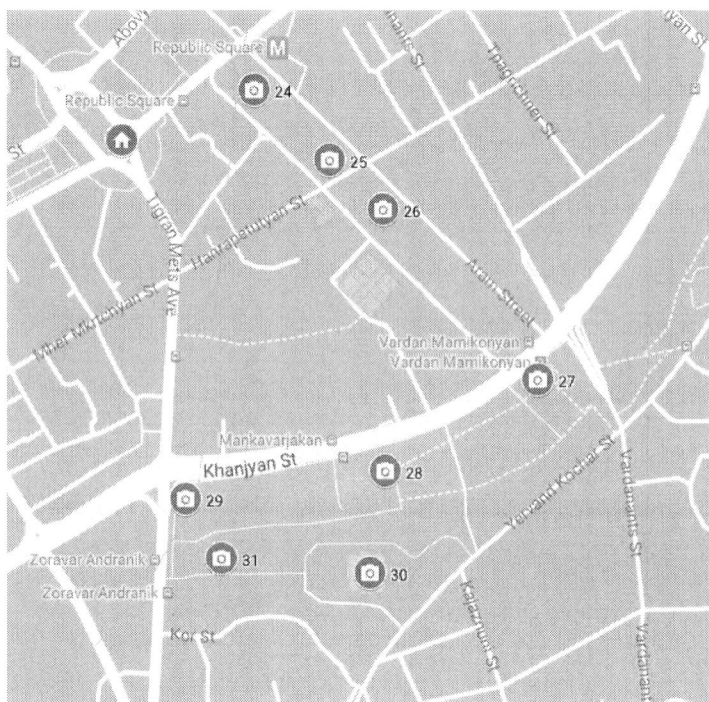

Map F: Aram Street to Zoravar Andranik Statue

Key:

24. *Aram Street and Park*

25. *Statue of Garegin Nzhdeh*

26. *Yerevan Vernissage*

27. *Vardan Mamikonian Statue*

28. *Circular Park*

29. *Statue of Alexander Griboyedov*

30. *Saint Gregory the Illuminator Cathedral*

31. *Zoravar Andranik Statue*

Aram Street and Park

Aram Street *(Map F, Point 24)* is one of the oldest in central Yerevan and takes its name from Aram Manukian, who was one of the founders of the First Republic of Armenia at the beginning of the twentieth century. Manukian also earned everlasting national hero status in 1915, after defending the Armenian population of Van against Ottoman Empire forces intent on committing genocide.

Most of the old buildings that lined this street have now disappeared, demolished in the 1990s to make way for modern residential and office blocks. The only remaining historic structures on this street are between the junctions of Abovyan Street and Mesrop Mashtots Avenue.

Today, there is a pleasant open square replete with fountains and lots of park benches under shady trees. It's a tranquil place to wander and relax in the heart of the city. Scattered around this space are many examples of khachkars, otherwise referred to as Armenian cross-stones. These steles were created to commemorate people (either living or dead), the construction of a church or a particularly notable military victory. You will notice that the majority of these have the same design elements: a cross, a rosette and a surrounding floral design of grapes, pomegranates, leaves and so on. Many were created in the medieval period, particularly between the twelfth and fourteenth centuries, and again during the sixteenth and seventeenth century when the artform experienced something of a renaissance. Examples from both periods stand in the park.

Walk through the park until you reach Hanrapetutyan Street.

* * *

Statue of Garegin Nzhdeh

The striking statue of the Armenian revolutionary and military leader, Garegin Nzhdeh *(Map F, Point 25)*, dominates the eastern end of the park. Armenians hold him in the highest regard, and participants in a recent television poll voted him to be the 'most outstanding figure' in Armenian history. In addition to this statue, a metro station, square and avenue in Yerevan take their name after this national hero.

Nzhdeh played a pivotal role in the national liberation struggle at the beginning of the twentieth century and participated in extensive revolutionary activities throughout World War I. This led to the eventual creation of the 1918-21 First Republic of Armenia, during which he had prominent roles. When the Soviets invaded Armenia, Nzhdeh established the anti-Bolshevik Republic of Mountainous Armenia, of which he was appointed Prime Minister. After months of fierce fighting with the Soviet authorities, he was eventually forced to capitulate and flee to Persia, where he continued political activism in exile throughout the 1930s. Towards the end of World War II, he discussed various plans with Soviet authorities to invade Turkey to punish them for their collaboration with the Nazis. The Soviets asked him to Moscow, after which he was promptly arrested for his counterrevolutionary activities back in the 1920s. He died in prison in 1955.

Cross Hanrapetutyan Street.

Yerevan Vernissage

The Vernissage *(Map F, Point 26)* is a 350 m-long open-air market running between Hanrapetutyan and Khanjyan Streets. It first began in the 1980s, when local artists used to display and sell their pieces in the park here. That is how the market got its name: Vernissage in French refers to the preview of an art exhibition.

These days paintings are still a prominent part of all the wares on display, although you can now find a vast array of souvenirs, handicrafts, carpets, jewellery, books, household items and odd assortments of bric-a-brac. It's a nice place to stroll around and pick up some bargains to remind you of your time in Armenia.

The market is open daily between 10 am and 6 pm. The best time to visit is during the mid-afternoon when most stalls will be open, and weekends will have the most vendors.

At the end of the Vernissage Market, turn left along Khanjyan Street, and directly in front of you will be a pedestrian underpass. Use this to cross the busy road.

Vardan Mamikonian statue

In the centre of a large open square is the domineering statue of Vardan Mamikonian *(Map F, Point 27)* on horseback. He was the fourth-century Armenian aristocrat, military leader and spiritual figurehead still revered to this day as the ultimate national hero.

Mamikonian was martyred on the battlefield while leading

the Armenian forces against the invading army of the Persian Sassanids on the Avarayr plain. While the Armenians lost this battle, resistance efforts continued, led by Mamikonian's nephew, Vahan. After thirty years of struggle, he eventually signed a treaty with the Persians guaranteeing religious freedom and enshrining their right to build new churches. So, the original battle came to be seen as a moral victory, and the day it was fought, 26 May, is celebrated every year as one of the most important holidays on the Armenian calendar. The Armenian Apostolic Church made Vardan a saint, and to this day Vardan remains a favourite boy's name.

From the statue, walk south along Khanjyan Street. To your left will be part of the Circular Park.

Circular Park

This park *(Map F, Point 28)* begins at the Poplavok lake near France Square, and arcs along the eastern edge of the Kentron district before coming to an end near Saint Gregory the Illuminator Cathedral. In total it stretches for two and a half kilometres, with a width of 120 m.

In this section of the park from the end of the Vernissage to the cathedral, there are many charming tea houses and cafes, a small lake and an amusement park.

Statue of Alexander Griboyedov

Marking the southern limit of the park, at the busy junction between Khanjyan Street and Tigran Mets Avenue, is a statue of diplomat, poet and composer Alexander Griboyedov *(Map*

F, Point 29).

During his time in the military, Griboyedov participated in many campaigns which aimed to liberate eastern Armenia from foreign forces and to incorporate it into the Russian Empire. Most notably he played a key role in ousting Persian troops from Yerevan Fortress in 1827.

In the aftermath of the Russo-Persian War, he was sent to Tehran as a diplomatic envoy, at a time when there was strong anti-Russian feeling there. Shortly after arriving, an Armenian eunuch escaped from the Shah's harem, and two enslaved Armenian women fled from the harem of the Shah's son-in-law. They all sought refuge at the Russian embassy. The shah demanded their release, yet Griboyedov refused, and as a result, an angry mob surrounded the diplomatic compound. When the protestors eventually broke in, Griboyedov and his legation valiantly fought back but were ultimately slaughtered. In an ignominious end, Griboyedov's body was thrown out of a window, decapitated and the head then displayed on a kebab stall for all to see. Today, his statue stands as a testament to his heroism in defending those helpless Armenian fugitives.

From the statue, turn left down Tigran Mets Avenue. After 50 m the Rossia Mall will be on your right, and the entrance to the Saint Gregory the Illuminator cathedral on the left.

Saint Gregory the Illuminator Cathedral

Saint Gregory the Illuminator Cathedral *(Map F, Point 30),* built between 1997 and 2001, is the largest Armenian cathedral in the world. Its construction was almost entirely funded through donations from prominent Armenian philanthropists and was designed to mark the 1700 years of

Christianity in Armenia.

The cathedral is dedicated to Saint Gregory the Illuminator, who is widely acknowledged to have converted Armenia from paganism to Christianity in 301, and houses his holy remains. One of the two smaller chapels within the cathedral takes its name from King Tiridates III, who proclaimed Christianity as the official state religion, and the other takes its name from his wife, Queen Ashkhen.

The height of the cathedral to the very top of its cross is 54 m, and the complex covers just a little less than 4000 square metres. At full capacity, it can hold two thousand worshippers.

Zoravar Andranik statue

As you walk back down the gently-sloping stairs from the cathedral to street level, you will see to your right a statue depicting Zoravar (General) Andranik *(Map F, Point 31)*, the military leader and best-known member of the *fedayi* Armenia militia groups. He led numerous armed campaigns against the Ottoman Empire forces at the end of the nineteenth century and continued this struggle right up to, and during, World War I, when he led Armenian volunteer forces into battle.

Andranik is greatly honoured throughout the country, and there are many other such statues. You will also see streets and squares named after him, and he features in songs and literature.

Once back on Tigran Mets Avenue, retrace your steps back to the junction with Khanjyan Street. Turn left along Agatangeghos Street, then take the first right, Movses Khorenatsi Street.

* * *

Capitals of the Caucasus

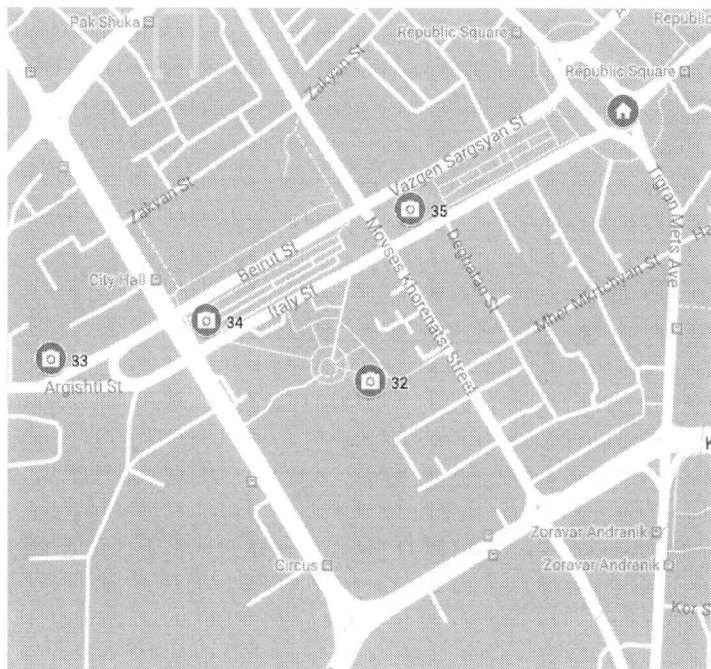

Map G: English Park to Shahumyan Park

Key:
  32. *English Park*
  33. *Yerevan History Museum*
  34. *Alexander Myasnikyan Statue*
  35. *Shahumyan Square and Park*

English Park

This 5.5-hectare leafy oasis *(Map G, Point 32)* in the middle of the city is one of the oldest parks in Yerevan, dating back to the 1860s. It is in the heart of the diplomatic district, with the embassies of France and Italy backing onto it. While in the

159

winter, when the trees are bare, the park can have a desolate feel to it, in the summer it is a beautiful place to relax and rest one's feet for a while.

At the very heart of the park, gazing out at the central fountain from under the trees, is a statue of Pepo, the hero of the Armenian 1930s film, which was itself an adaptation of Gabriel Sundukyan's 1876 play. The film, which follows the struggle of a poor, honest Armenian fisherman against a scheming trader, is now considered to be one of the best pre-World War II Soviet films. In recognition of Sundukyan's significant contribution to Armenian culture, the National Academic Theatre adjacent to the park is named after him.

Exit the park on its western side, by taking the path that runs alongside the Gabriel Sundukyan Theatre. Turn right along Grigor Lusavorich Street. At the junction with Argishti Street turn left, and the Yerevan History Museum will be on your right after about 100 m.

Yerevan History Museum

Yerevan is one of the oldest continuously inhabited cities in the world, having been established way back in the mists of time during the eighth century BC. The Yerevan History Museum *(Map G, Point 33)* presents every stage of this long story, through its collection of 94,000 exhibits. These include a vast array of archaeological finds, art, coins, textiles, weapons, furniture, photos and much more besides.

The museum has three major halls, each one dealing with a big chunk of history. The first looks at everything from prehistoric times up to the medieval period, the second tells the story of the nineteenth century and growing Russian imperialism, and the last hall examines the twentieth-century history of Armenia and ultimately the attainment of its independence.

The museum is open from Monday to Saturday, from 11 am to 5.30 pm, and is closed on Sundays. The entrance fee is 500 AMD, and foreign language guided tours are available for 3000 AMD.

From the museum, walk up Beirut Street back towards Republic Square. After 100 m, at the intersection with Grigor Lusavorich Street, you will be in Myasnikyan Square.

Alexander Myasnikyan statue

Facing you, and dominating the square, is the monument to Alexander Myasnikyan *(Map G, Point 34)*, one of the greatest Bolsheviks of Armenian origins. He was more popularly known by his revolutionary nickname, Martuni.

After the creation of the Soviet Union, Myasnikyan became a senior leader in the newly-formed Armenian Soviet Socialist Republic. During his tenure, he played an instrumental role in setting up government institutions and enthusiastically set about eradicating illiteracy and boosting the local economy.

Myasnikyan came to a premature end in 1925 in a mysterious plane crash. While some thought it just an unfortunate accident, others claim that it was a state-sponsored assassination. Whatever the truth, Myasnikyan is one of the very few communist leaders that remain popular to this day.

Walk behind the statue and continue straight. This landscaped area running between Beirut and Italy Streets runs for 200 m up to Shahumyan Square.

* * *

Shahumyan Square and Park

Pride of place in the centre of this square is an imposing statue of Stepan Shahumyan *(Map G, Point 35)*, an ethnic Armenian and prominent Bolshevik who led the Russian Revolution in the Caucasus. Due to his revolutionary activities across the region, he earned the nickname 'Caucasian Lenin'.

Shahumyan eventually became head of the shortlived Baku Commune which continued the spread of the revolution in the Caucasus region. His tenure faced many problems, from ethnic strife to invading Turkish forces. However, he generally took a considered and diplomatic approach to solving these crises and did not readily resort to violence as many of his Bolshevik counterparts were known to do. The Baku Commune was ousted in July 1918, prompting Shahumyan and other leaders to flee into exile. However, anti-Bolshevik forces managed to capture them in September of the same year and executed them on the spot.

Today, in addition to this statue, many streets and towns across the ex-Soviet Union are named in his honour. And behind this statue, the park that runs right up to Republic Square also takes its name from the great revolutionary. Along its entire length, restaurants line either side of burbling fountains, and it is a particularly pleasant place for lunch, dinner or an evening stroll during the summer months.

Continue walking through the park. You will eventually get back to Republic Square, where this walking tour comes to an end.

Yerevan Walking Tour 3 - Wandering around the west of Yerevan

This tour takes in the sights to the west of Republic Square.

Walk south from Republic Square through Shahumyan Park. Continue down Beirut Street, then turn right along Grigor Lusavorich Street. Where it forks into two, take Paronyan Street to the left. Then walk down the first turning on the left, Dzoragyugh 1st Street, past the Lebanese Embassy and the museum will be on your right.

* * *

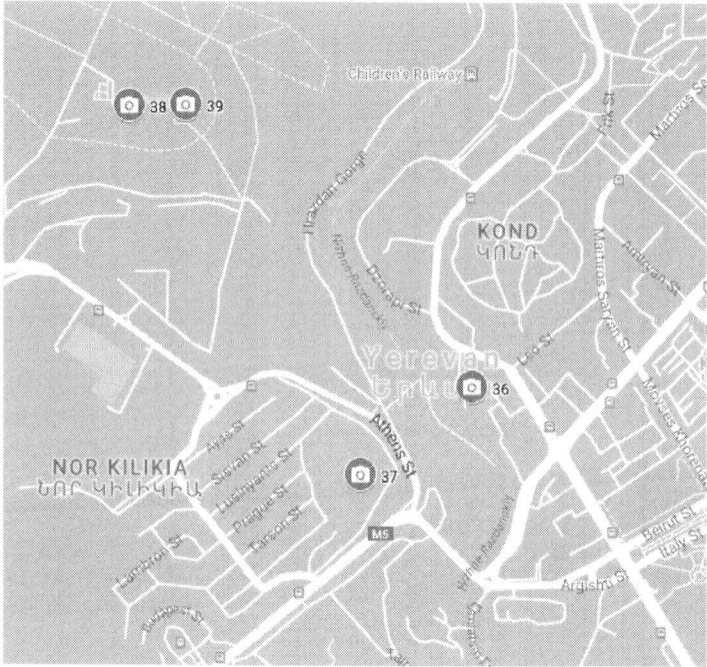

Map H: Sergei Parajanov Museum to Tsiternakaberd

Key:

36. Sergei Parajanov Museum
37. Yerevan Brandy Company and ArArAt Museum
38. Armenian Genocide Museum
39. Tsiternakaberd

Sergei Parajanov Museum

While you might not have heard of Sergei Parajanov before visiting Yerevan, a visit to this off-the-beaten-track museum *(Map H, Point 36)* is well worth the effort. Parajanov was a Soviet-born Armenian film director and prolific artist. He selected these premises just outside Kentron district, intending to live in one part and dedicate the other to a museum of his work. The 1988 earthquake delayed the project, and the museum eventually opened in 1990 one year after his death.

Parajanov was born in Tbilisi, Georgia, in 1924 to Armenian parents. After an early education that focused on the arts, particularly music, song and dance, he moved to Moscow to attend the Institute of Cinema, where some of the great Russian filmmakers taught him. He graduated in 1951, and it wasn't long before he began to create his own films. His first masterpiece was the 1964 film *Shadows of Forgotten Ancestors*, which earnt him international acclaim. Parajanov's most revered masterpiece, which some critics claim is among the best films ever made, was the 1969 *Colour of Pomegranates*, a biographical account of the Armenian poet Sayat Nova.

However, at around this time, his films attracted the attention of the Soviet authorities and were subject to severe censorship. His relationship with the powers-that-be deteriorated further, and Parajanov's outspoken criticism of Soviet cinema eventually saw him imprisoned for much of the 1970s. During his time locked away, he still worked hard on producing other artwork, many examples of which the museum displays today. After his release in 1977, and throughout the next decade, his artistic output increased even further and broadened into many other genres.

The museum's collection comprises 1500 individual pieces, including a diverse range of collages, drawings, film sketches, dolls, hats and screenplays. A separate room showcases the work Parajanov produced in prison. Two memorial rooms display Parajanov's personal effects, as well as prizes, posters and letters from luminaries such as Fellini.

It is open every day of the week from 10.30 am to 5 pm. The entrance fee is 1000 AMD, and guided tours are available for 2500 AMD.

Retrace your steps down Paronyan Street to its junction with Mesrop Mashtots Avenue. Turn right, and after 200 m turn right again on to Victory Bridge. As you cross the gorge, you will see the Yerevan Brandy Company on top of the hill in fromt of you. To access the site, walk up the hill using the grand double staircase.

Yerevan Brandy Company and ArArAt Museum

You can't miss the imposing bulk of the Yerevan Brandy Company's factory *(Map H, Point 37)*, set high up on a slope overlooking Victory Bridge and the Hrazdan valley, with its famous brand name ArArAt emblazoned across it. The good news is that the factory is open to visitors curious about this most Armenian of drinks.

You begin your visit at the Ararat Museum, from where all the guided tours start. Visitors get to learn about the history of the company, all the different types of ArArAt brandies, and get to see and smell the vast cellars packed with barrels. There is even one very special barrel which will remain stoppered until peace breaks out between Armenia and Azerbaijan. However, the highlight for most visitors is the tasting of the brandies, which comes after the tour at an additional cost of 10,000 AMD.

The Armenian merchant Nerses Tairov founded the brandy company in 1887, and the reputation of the brandy spread so quickly and so far that by the turn of the century the factory was supplying the Imperial court of Russia. Also at this time, the brandy received such high acclaim at the 1900 Internation Exhibition in Paris that it earned the right to be called 'cognac'. Many famous figures throughout recent history have been ArArAt drinkers, including Sir Winston Churchill,

Agatha Christie and Frank Sinatra. Churchill had his first taste of the brandy in 1945 at the Yalta conference, and in the following years received a case each month from Stalin.

In 1953, following a corporate reorganisation, the Yerevan Brandy Company relocated to its present site. With its brick facade, nine minimalist arches and grand staircases leading up the hillside, the complex is regarded as one of the best examples of Soviet architecture in the whole country.

In the years following Armenian independence, the company became state-owned, and in 1998 was sold to the giant drinks manufacturer Pernod Ricard for USD 30 million. Today, its products are exported to 25 countries, although the Russian market accounts for the lion's share of this business.

The cognac brands produced range from a six-year-old ArArAt *Ani* to the ArArAt *Erebuni* at 30 years old. At the end of your tour, you can visit an onsite shop, although tourists report that prices are lower at the Yerevan Zvartnots Airport duty-free shop.

The museum is open every day from 9 am to 8 pm, and tours can be reserved online at en.araratbrandy.com.

The quickest and easiest way to the next stop, the Armenian Genocide Museum, is to hop in a taxi for the short 1 km ride up the hill. By foot, follow Athens Street up past Hrazdan Stadium. Here the road becomes the Tsiternakaberd Highway. When you see the Dalma Mall, the service road leading up to the museum will be a further 200 m on your right.

Armenian Genocide Museum

The Armenian Genocide Museum *(Map H, Point 38)* was opened in 1995 to mark the eightieth anniversary of the 1915 genocide. It tells the story of this horrific period, during which one and a half million Armenians living in the Ottoman Empire lost their lives, and a further half a million experienced conversion to Islam or exile.

Twelve halls present the story of the genocide, from the earliest beginnings of human rights abuses against Armenians in the nineteenth century, through to the events of the eight-year-long massacre between 1915-1923. All of this mass of information is broken down into fifty-two individual sub-headings, spread in chronological order throughout the halls. To illustrate each there are a variety of artefacts, including print materials, photos, videos, maps, multimedia displays and original official documents. It's vital that this genocide is never forgotten, and by increasing awareness of it, the museum helps to ensure that such a terrible period of history is less likely to occur again.

The museum is open Tuesdays to Sundays from 11 am to 5 pm. It closes on Mondays. There is no entrance fee, although donations are welcome.

Tsiternakaberd

A short distance from the museum is the strikingly poignant Tsiternakaberd memorial *(Map H, Point 39)*, opened in 1965 and dedicated to the victims of the genocide. It takes its name from the hill on which it stands, and its prominent position ensures that anyone in the city below can see it. This site has witnessed a lot of history over the centuries, due to its strategic location with far-reaching views over the Hrazdan river valley, and has been home to iron age forts, Roman apartments, medieval structures and there are even traces of Neolithic settlements.

The memorial comprises a 44-metre high needle-like stele which represents the rebirth of the Armenian nation after the trauma of the 1915 genocide. While the needle symbolises national unity, it has a deep cleft which reminds people that the violence of the genocide also caused their dispersion around the world. Surrounding this are twelve inward-leaning basalt slabs, each symbolising Armenian provinces lost to Turkey, and under their shadow, in an inner courtyard, an eternal flame burns in memory of the 1.5 million victims. Once inside this memorial, you hear Armenian classical music and will likely see many flowers placed by local people still paying tribute to their lost family members.

Leading up to the memorial is a one hundred metre-long wall, upon which are inscribed the names of the towns and villages where atrocities took place. On the other side, you can see plaques commemorating those who selflessly dedicated themselves to helping victims during that time.

Vagharshapat UNESCO World Heritage Sites

The UNESCO World Heritage Sites located in and around Vagharshapat make for a comfortable half-day trip from Yerevan. The easiest way to get there would be to hire a taxi, and there is no shortage of willing drivers who would be more than happy to take you out there. The first stop on the way out of Yerevan city proper is Zvartnots Cathedral, just a little way past the international airport.

* * *

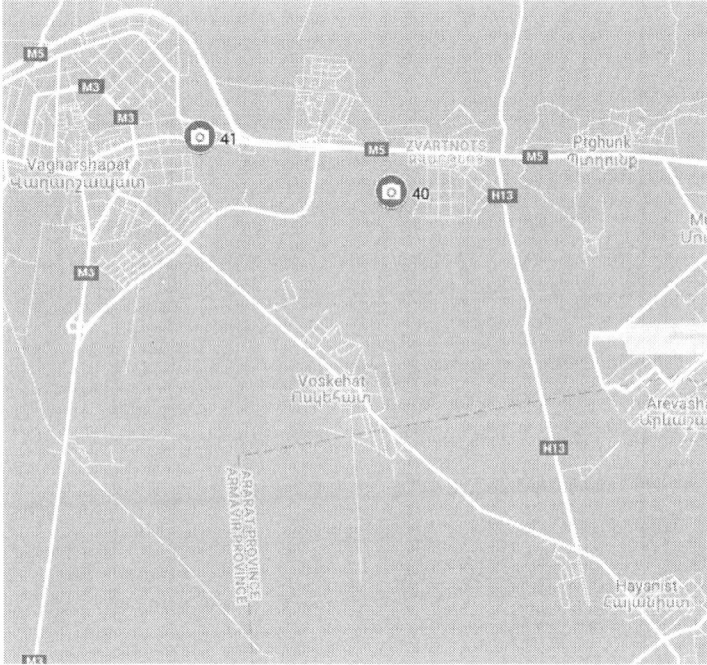

Map I: Zvartnots Cathedral and Saint Hripsime Church

Key:
  40. Zvartnots Cathedral
  41. Saint Hripsime Church

Zvartnots Cathedral

When you first reach the semi-industrial, semi-derelict landscape, just at the end of the runway of the international airport, you might think that this is an unlikely place for a UNESCO World Heritage Site. However, you will quickly understand when you enter the compound of the ruins of Zvartnots Cathedral *(Map I, Point 40)* and catch your first glimpse of its arches framing the snow-capped Mount Ararat. Zvartnots is a monument which shows just how advanced Armenian architects were at a time when much of Europe languished in the Dark Ages, and you can see clear evidence of both engineering excellence and artistic flair.

Construction of the cathedral began in 643 on the order of the Patriarch of the Armenian church, Catholicos Nerses III, who was nicknamed 'the builder' due to his ambitious construction projects. It stands on the spot of the first meeting between Saint Gregory the Illuminator, who first converted Armenians to Christianity, with then-king Tiridates III. The cathedral's consecration took place after just nine short years of construction in 652.

For more than three hundred years Zvartnots Cathedral stood proudly, yet in the tenth century was mysteriously destroyed, with scholars surmising that the cause might have been a massive earthquake or marauding Arab invaders. Whatever the reason for its downfall, its ruins slowly subsumed into the ground, where they remained right up until the twentieth century, when the ecclesiastic Khachik Dadyan began excavations. Years of archaeological work unearthed much of the stonework of the cathedral, which enabled the prominent Armenian architect and historian, Toros Tormanian, to partially rebuild the church into the structure you see today.

The interior structure was in the form of a tetraconch, with four equally-sized apses forming the plan of a Greek cross; in the centre of this were the buried remains of Saint Gregory the Illuminator. This inner part of the temple was then encircled by an aisle, separating it from the external walls, which had 32 sides making the cathedral appear circular from a distance. While the remains you see today derive from the lower parts of the structure, the church had three tiers which would have towered over the surrounding countryside.

Rich decorations covered the cathedral, and you can see tantalising glimpses of such ornamentation when you walk around the ruins. Keep your eyes open for carved pomegranates, symbolising fertility, and grapes representing the blood of God and resurrection. Carved eagles signify strength and victory. The thirty-two master stone masons had their portraits cut into the thirty-two sides of the cathedral; nine remain today.

Slightly to the southwest of the cathedral, you can find the ruins of the Catholicos Palace, where the head of the Armenian Church, Nerses III, lived and worked. Today, only the lowermost segments of the walls are visible, but these give you a good idea of how the palace might have appeared. It had two main wings. The western wing comprised two main spaces, the Hall of Columns and the Winter Hall, grand venues for receptions and events. The eastern wing held various living quarters for the clergy, a throne room and a Roman bath. Alongside the palace is a small winery.

There is a small museum towards the rear of the site, and this showcases some of the best stone carvings and other ancient artefacts. There are many information boards giving details on all the past excavations. Most useful are the scale models of how the cathedral looked like in its heyday, and to get the most out of your visit it would be a good idea first to visit this museum, and then wander around the ruins.

The most convenient way of reaching this site is by taxi, combining the visit with a trip to the sights in Vagharshapat. Alternatively, you can take the N111 minibus from Yerevan's Kilikia Avtokayan bus station. Zvartnots cathedral is open every day between 9 am and 5.30pm. The entrance fee is 700 AMD.

Saint Hripsime Church

Saint Hripsime Church *(Map I, Point 41)*, the next UNESCO World Heritage Site in this area, is a just a couple of kilometres along the main M5 highway from Zvartnots Cathedral, in the outskirts of Vagharshapat. It is one of the oldest churches still standing in Armenia, dating back to the seventh century, and contains the remains of Saint Hripsime.

To determine the origins of this church we need to look back to Roman times in the third century. Scholars believe that Hripsine was a noblewoman who was part of a community of thirty-five virgin nuns in Rome. She was supposedly extremely beautiful, to such an extent that she attracted the unwanted attention of Emperor Diocletian. Eventually, Hripsime and her entire community fled, first to Egypt and then to Vagharshapat. Unfortunately, history proceeded to repeat itself, with the then-Armenian king, Tiridates III, becoming captivated by her beauty. She rebuffed his advantages, and the infuriated king punished her by roasting her alive with all but one of her fellow maidens. Parts of this story seem to be rooted in fact, as recent excavations have found early Christian burials of tortured women.

The legend then relates how the king quickly became ill and started wandering the forest adopting the behaviour of a wild boar. The king was taken to the cell of Gregory the Illuminator, whom he had imprisoned years earlier, and received a miraculous cure. Then Tiridates III, who had seen the power of God at work at first hand, promptly declared that Armenia should adopt Christianity. In repentance, the king built a small church at the site of Hripsime's martyrdom, to house the saint's remains. Following a Persian invasion, this was then rebuilt in 395 by Catholicos Sahak the Great.

Catholicos Komitas constructed the current building in 618, and this seventh-century structure has remained pretty much untouched over the intervening centuries. Indeed, it received so little attention that by the seventeenth century it was a rather lonely abandoned structure that prompted the then-Catholicos to embark on a renovation programme. In the eighteenth century saw the addition of the bell tower and defensive walls.

Architecturally, the church is a domed tetraconch, with four equally-sized apses enclosed in a rectangle. Its exterior is austerely beautiful, with the great blocks of masonry relatively untouched by any decorative flourishes. Scholars have deemed the structure to be one of the most significant of Armenian medieval architecture. In recognition of its superlative architecture, similar churches around the country are now referred to 'Hripsime-type'.

The interior is dark and atmospheric, and you get a real feel for just how many centuries the church has stood. To the right of the altar, you can find stone steps leading down into the catacombs, where a small chamber holds the remains of Saint Hripsime.

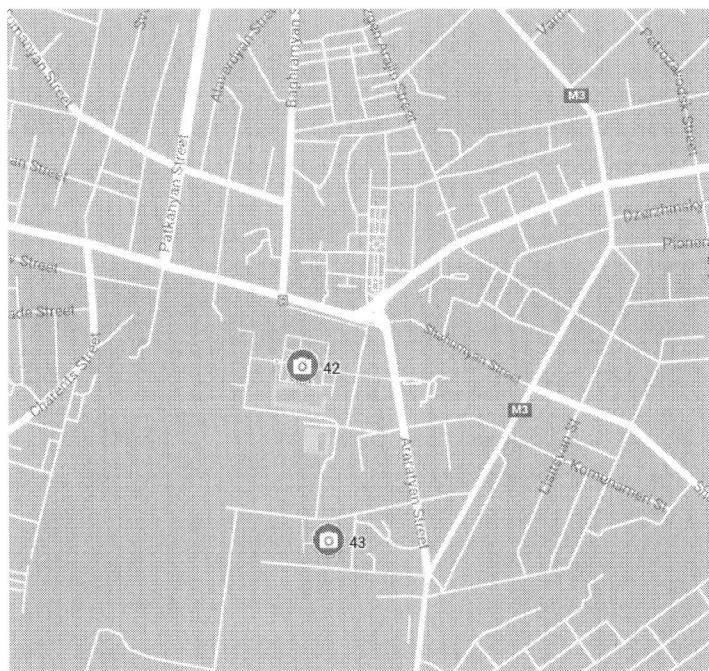

Map J: Etchmiadzin Cathedral and Saint Gayane Church

Key:
  42. *Etchmiadzin Cathedral*
  43. *Saint Gayane Church*

Etchmiadzin Cathedral

Located right in the heart of Vagharashapat is the Etchmiadzin Cathedral *(Map J, Point 42)*, the mother church of the Armenian Apostolic Church. According to some scholars, this is the oldest cathedral in the world, and for an astonishing seventeen centuries has stood at the epicentre of Armenia's religious and cultural life. It's safe to say that this is the Armenian equivalent of the Vatican. This importance was recognised by UNESCO in 2000 when it added the cathedral to its register of World Heritage Sites.

As with other churches of significance, the cathedral rests on the remains of a much earlier pagan temple. Legend has it that the site was chosen as a result of a vision of Armenia's patron saint, Gregory the Illuminator, in which he saw Jesus come down from the heavens and strike the earth with a golden hammer indicating the desired site for the church. Indeed, the name Etchmiadzin roughly translates from Armenian as 'descent of the son of God'. In the late fifth century this original cathedral was severely damaged during a Persian invasion, and so was almost entirely built from the foundations upwards in 483/4.

The church you see today is the result. It was dramatically different in design from its predecessor, having a square shaped plan enclosing a Greek cross. There were four apses, circular inside and polygonal outside, and two chapels to either side of the eastern apse. The four columns supporting the dome neatly divide the main body of the church into nine squares of equal area.

In the many following centuries, Etchmiadzin cathedral underwent successive waves of neglect, looting by invading forces and renovation. The last piece of major reconstruction was in 1868 when Catholicos George IV built a sacristy around the easternmost end of the church.

As with Saint Hripsime church and other religious buildings in Armenia, the exterior of the core fifth century part of the church is quite austere and unostentatious. Later architectural additions, such as the belfry and cupola, have some geometric and floral carvings. Inside, there are many frescoes, and particularly striking are those inside the dome and belfry. The earliest examples were renovated in the eighteenth century, and further frescoes showing various saints and scenes from the Old Testament were added throughout the eighteenth and nineteenth centuries.

If you would like to participate in one of the morning services, they are held at 7.30 am, except for Sundays when it is at 8 am. Daily evening services are at 5.30 pm. The Divine Liturgy on Sunday starts from 11 am.

Etchmiadzin Cathedral Museum

The museum is within the walls of the cathedral itself, inside the sacristy added during the latter half of the nineteenth century. The entrance is to the right of the altar. You need a ticket to enter the museum, and these are not available for purchase inside the cathedral. So before you begin your visit, go to the ground floor of the Palace of the Catholicos, directly opposite the main door of the cathedral; there should be signs pointing the way to the ticket desk.

Once inside the museum, you can view more than three thousand religious artefacts displayed throughout the grand exhibition halls. There are a lot of thought-provoking pieces, and when you read the English labels alongside each, you are sometimes taken aback by what is purportedly on show. There is a piece of wood from the cross of Christ, fragments from Noah's Ark which came to rest on the nearby Mount Ararat, and a bit of the lance that a Roman soldier used to piece Jesus when he was on the cross. In addition to these headline exhibits, there is a dazzling array of ritual objects, religious vestments such as mitres, crowns and intricately-embroidered robes, paintings, illustrated manuscripts and bibles.

The museum is open daily from 10.30 am to 5 pm, except on Sundays when it opens at 1.30pm after the completion of Divine Liturgy. The entrance fee is 1500 AMD.

Saint Gayane Church

A short walk to the south of the Etchmiadzin Cathedral complex is the Saint Gayane church *(Map J, Point 43)*, the third UNESCO World Heritage Site in Vagharshapat. To get here, walk out of the eastern gate, turn right and walk along Araratyan Street for about 300 m until its junction with Issy-les-Moulineaux Street. Turn right, and the entrance to the church will be on your left a bit further along. This site receives far fewer visitors than the others, and you may have the place to yourself.

The church was built in the seventh century on the site where Saint Gayane was martyred at the very beginning of the fourth century. Gayane was the abbesse that was in charge of Hripsime and the other nuns that had fled to Armenia to escape from Emperor Diocletian. King Tiridates had fallen in love with both Hripsime, and later Gayane, yet they both rebuffed his advances. While King Tiridates tortured and killed Hripsime where the Saint Hripsime Church stands today, he murdered Gayane on this spot.

Architecturally, Saint Gayane Church is a three-nave basilica with a cruciform plan. It is made from a reddish-brown tuff, a locally-found volcanic rock, which gives it a warm, welcoming appearance. Its octagonal drum is supported by four pillars, which split the interior into the three naves. The distinctive triple-arched portico is a late seventeenth-century addition, and when you enter the church look out for the beautiful fresco above the door.

Day Trips from Yerevan

Day trip from Yerevan - 1: Garni Temple and the Monasteries of Geghard and Sevanavank

An easy half-day trip east from Yerevan takes in the ancient religious sites of the Garni Temple and the Geghard Monastery. It is advisable to rent a taxi for this excursion, as public transport does not provide any convenient options.

* * *

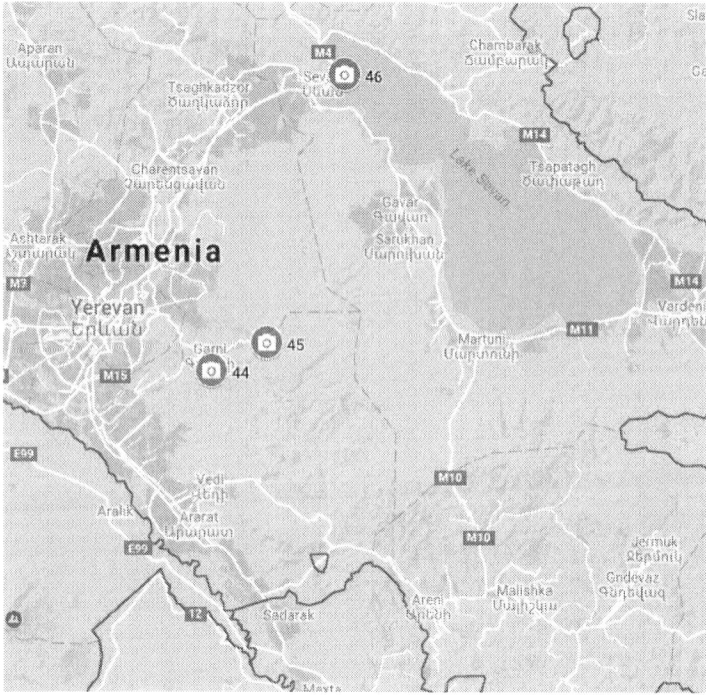

Map K: Garni Temple, Geghard and Sevanovank Monasteries

Key:
  44. *Garni Temple*
  45. *Geghard Monastery*
  46. *Sevanovank Monastery*

Garni Temple

Perched high up on a rocky headland overlooking the Azat River, is the spectacular first-century Garni Temple *(Map K, Point 44)*, the most significant structure from the pre-Christian era in the whole country. Scholars believe that King Tiridates

Capitals of the Caucasus

I of Armenia built the temple, and while the exact date is subject to debate, it is safe to identify it as a first-century structure because Roman historian Tacitus wrote about it in his *Annals*.

Scholars believe that this pagan temple was dedicated to the sun-god Mihr, who was considered by the king to be the patron-God of Armenia. However, when King Tiridates III embraced Christianity in the early fourth century, the fortunes for such pagan structures quickly took a turn for the worst. Almost every single pagan place of worship was destroyed, yet Garni was inexplicably spared, possibly due to its artistic merit or that it also acted as a tomb.

During the following centuries, some modifications were made to the temple, and the royal family used it as a kind of summer house. It remained standing until 1679 when a devastating earthquake caused the temple to collapse, leaving behind a confused jumble of stone. It laid in a state of ruin until the 1960s, when the Soviet authorities decided to rebuild it. Luckily, more than eighty per cent of the stone remained on site, and the temple was rebuilt using these original stones. If a piece was missing, the renovators used stones of a different type so that the modern reconstructions could be readily recognised.

In architectural terms, Garni is a peripteros, meaning that a portico with twenty-four columns surrounds the inner temple, with the entire structure built on a raised platform. The steps of the staircase leading up to the front of the temple are very high, designed so that people had to make a real physical effort to get to the temple, and so humbling them in the process. The triangular pediment at the front of the temple shows plants and geometric shapes, and the frieze surrounding the temple depicts acanthus flowers.

Today, this UNESCO World Heritage site is one of the major tourist attractions of Armenia, and the temple often forms the backdrop for significant cultural events. It's a must-see for any international visitor to Armenia.

Geghard monastery

A further ten kilometres down the road from the Garni temple is the Geghard monastery *(Map K, Point 45)*. This religious complex was established by the patron saint of Armenia, Gregory the Illuminator and dates back as far as the fourth century. However, most of the historic structures on this site today are medieval and date from the thirteenth century.

'Geghard' roughly translates as 'monastery of the spear'. Stored here for centuries was the lance that purportedly was used by a Roman soldier to pierce the side of Jesus Christ while on the cross. Today, this relic resides in the museum at Echmiadzin cathedral, yet despite this, the monastery remains one of the top tourist destinations in the country

The monastery is in a spectacular gorge at the very end of the highway, and high cliffs encircle it. To get to the complex, you have to walk uphill, past hordes of souvenir sellers, and while climbing keep your eyes out for holes in the cliff face which are ancient hand-hewn cells for resident monks.

Once through the main entrance and inside the monastic compound, the most prominent structure facing you is the **vestry** of the Katoghike Chapel, with the main church just behind it. Upon entering the vestry, referred to as a *gavit* in Armenian, you get a real taste of antiquity; its construction took place between 1215 and 1225. Four massive columns hold up a dome adorned with beautiful stalactites. A hole in the centre of the dome allows the entry of natural light into the gavit. This space would have been used for receiving pilgrims and for religious teaching.

On the far side of the gavit is the entrance into the main **Katoghike Chapel** itself, built in 1215 under the patronage of two generals of Queen Tamar of Georgia. The plan of the church is the traditional Armenian form of an equally-armed cross within a square. The southern facade of the church is particularly ornately carved around the door, with many intricate representations of pomegranates, grapes and doves.

Back in the vestry, you will find in the northwestern corner an entrance into the first totally rock-hewn church, the **Avazan**. This chamber was cut in the 1240s, and inside there is a natural spring with supposedly holy water. Even today you will see many people eagerly filling up empty bottles with the lucky water.

During the thirteenth century, the princes of the Proshian dynasty, a notable Armenian aristocratic family, bought the monastery. They accelerated the development of the complex, and in a few short years built a second church inside the mountain, a study hall, monastic cells and family tombs.

Back in the gavit, this time in the northeastern corner, you can find your way into the **Zhamatun**, which is another rock-hewn chamber that is the tomb of the Proshian princes. Various wall carvings depict lions and dragons, and the eagle with half-spread wings is likely to have been the coat of arms of the princes.

The tomb gives way to a rock-cut chamber called the **St. Astvatsatsin Church**. Thanks to an inscription, we can pinpoint the construction of this church at precisely 1283, and it was paid for by the Proshian princes. It took a staggering forty years to complete its carving out, which was done by hand from the top-down. Representations of animals, warriors, crosses and some floral elements decorate the walls. The prominent cracks you see result from some of the massive earthquakes that have rocked Armenia over time, the last being in 1679.

To access the final chamber deep inside the rock of the cliffside, the **Upper Zhamatun**, you need to go back out into the courtyard. Near the door of the gavit (the first building you entered) is a small staircase leading uphill. In a scene straight out of an Indian Jones movie, you follow a mysterious rock-hewn corridor covered in crosses. Once inside the chamber, you will see four stout columns, which hold up the dome and divide the space into nine equal parts. This was originally the resting place of Prince Prosh's son and his son's wife. You'll notice that the acoustics are outstanding here, and this chamber was also likely used for the singing of Armenian religious songs called *sharakans*. In the corner of this chamber, there is a small hole which connects with the lower rock-hewn chambers, and this probably was cut so that the chanting could carry through the whole complex of rooms.

Once you have finished touring the Geghard, exit through a small door in the rear wall, and you will emerge next to a fast stream flowing down the mountainside, choked with large boulders. Cross the picturesque arched bridge and walk down the opposite bank for 50 m and you will come to a matagh, a sacrificial site recognisable by small stone cairns. This area is used on Sundays after the main service has finished. While walking down there, you'll notice prayer flags tied to the branches of overhanging trees; apparently, if you say a prayer, make a wish and tie a piece of cloth on the trees next to the monastery, it will come true.

As an extension to the Garni temple / Geghard Monastery half-day trip, you can also journey up to the Sevanovank monastery. Perched on a peninsula jutting out into the blue waters of Lake Sevan, this is one of the most iconic historical sites of Armenia. Your driver will need to backtrack almost all the way back to Yerevan, before turning onto the M4 highway for about an hour's drive to the lake.

Sevanavank Monastery

Today, this spectacularly-situated monastic complex *(Map K, Point 46)* is now easily accessible, although this wasn't always the case. The two surviving churches, the Surp Arakelots (Holy Apostles) and Surp Astvatsatsin (Holy Mother of God) were initially on an island, cut off from the mainland by the waters of Lake Sevan. When Stalin ordered the artificial draining of the lake, the water level fell a dramatic 20 m, exposing the narrow strip of land which transformed the island into a peninsula. Today, the government is making efforts to raise the water level once more, so Sevanavank could potentially reclaim its island status in the coming years.

The monastery was founded in the ninth century by Princess Mariam, daughter of King Ashot the First. Due to its original isolated location, the monastery acted as a place of temporary exile for monks from Etchmiadzin who had sinned in some way. Wine, women and meat were all strictly prohibited. The Saint Astvatsatsin church used to serve as a repository of gifts sent to the monastery such as manuscripts, books, jewellery and crosses.

The churches take the same architectural form, although one is smaller than the other. Both have a cruciform plan, with an octagonal drum topped by an octagonal dome. The construction material is locally-sourced black volcanic tuff. Nearby the churches are the foundations of a gavit, some remains of which can be seen in the Yerevan Museum of History.

There are many interesting theories regarding the name 'Sevan'. The less romantic of these is that it is the word simply means 'lake' in the Urartian language spoken by ancient inhabitants in this region. A somewhat more grisly theory is that Sevan is a combination of the Armenian word Sev (Black) and Van (Lake), as in a battle King Ashot killed so many Arabs here that the waters appeared black. A final possibility is that the name derives from 'black monastery' (Sev-Vank) after the dark volcanic rock used to build the churches. Whatever the etymology, the views of the lake and the surrounding mountain ranges are truly awe-inspiring and are worth the trip alone. The best panoramas are from near the tip of the peninsula, and this is where the Armenian presidential summer house is quite wisely located down near the water.

On your way back down to the car park, you will encounter many souvenir sellers, so this might be a good place to stock up instead of paying inflated airport prices. Also down by the shoreline you can book boat tours of the lake of varying lengths. For adrenaline seekers, it is also possible to jump off a nearby mountaintop and go paragliding over the lake, getting a fabulous aerial view of the monastery at the same time.

Day trip from Yerevan - 2: Norovank and Khor Virap

The journey to the south and southeast of Yerevan to Norovank and Khor Virap monasteries is a comfortable day trip. You can visit the two religious sites in either order; Khor Virap is around forty-five minutes from Yerevan, while Norovank is a further hour and fifteen minutes down the road.

* * *

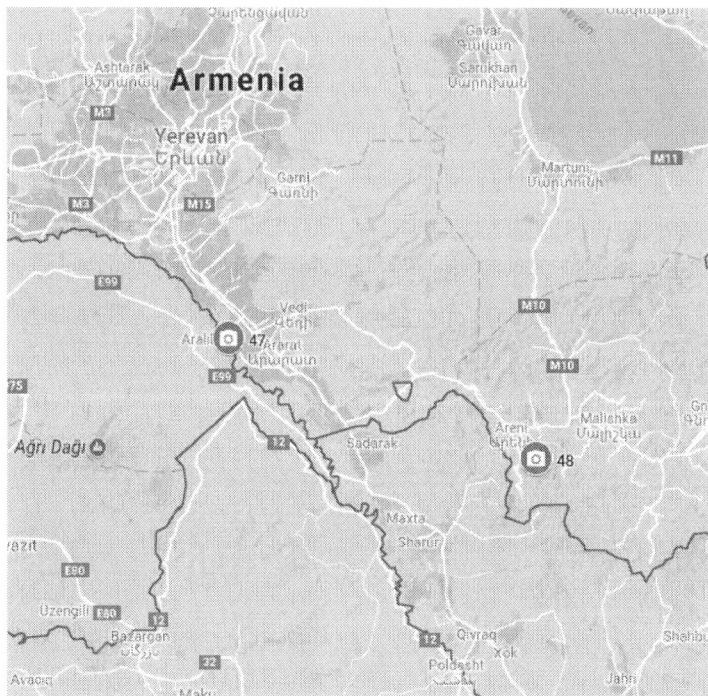

Map L: Khor Virap and Norovank Monasteries

Key:
   47. Khor Virap Monastery
   48. Norovank Monastery

Khor Virap

The Khor Virap monastery *(Map L, Point 47)* is situated up close (a mere 100 m) with the long-closed Turkish border on the Ararat plain. Mount Ararat itself forms an imposing backdrop to the spectacularly-located religious complex and accordingly features prominently on Armenian postcards and tourist websites.

In the third century, way before churches were built here, Khor Virap acted as a Royal prison. The reason this site became religiously significant is that Gregory the Illuminator, who subsequently became the patron saint of Armenia, was imprisoned here for thirteen long years. At the end of the third century, the then-King, Tiridates III, was a pagan, and the proselytising activities of Gregory led to his incarceration in this remote and inhospitable jail. His cell was at the bottom of a deep shaft, and Khor Virap roughly translates as 'bottom-most pit'. He miraculously survived and was released when Tiridates III needed to be cured of his insanity, which as we previously saw occurred after killing Hripsime and the nuns. Because of Gregory's divine powers, as the king saw them, Tiridates then did a rapid about turn and became a passionate advocate for Christianity, resulting in the country adopting the religion in 301.

As a mark of reverence to Saint Gregory, the Catholicos of the Armenian Apostolic Church, Nerses III, built a chapel at Khor Virap in 642. Due to its strategic location, the church suffered from the looting and vandalism of a succession of invading forces and was rebuilt several times over the centuries. The church you see today, called St. Astvatsatsin (Holy Mother of God) dates from 1662, and it was at this time that saw the construction of the surrounding defensives walls, so creating an inner courtyard.

This church is constructed around the ruins of the earlier chapels and is also built over the pit where Gregory was imprisoned so long ago. While the church takes the traditional Armenian plan of a cross within a square, it is unusually aligned northwest-southeast instead of the more common east-west direction. To the right of the alter you can climb down to the famous dungeon using a metal ladder. It gets sweltering down there in the summer and gives you just a small taste of the punishment given to Gregory all those years ago. Back outside, you can walk up a small hillock, and its peak affords panoramic views of Khor Virap and the majestic Mount Ararat.

Norovank

Norovank *(Map L, Point 48)* is about 90 km from Khor Virap, in the narrow gorge of the Amaghi river. This monastery was a major religious centre and seat of learning during the thirteenth and fourteenth centuries, and home to the Orbelians, local aristocrats. Norovank is most famous for its two-storey Surb Astvatsatsin Church, along with the smaller Surb Karapet Church and adjoining Surb Grigor Chapel. The surrounding fortified walls were built during the seventeenth and eighteenth centuries.

Prince Burtel Orbelian financed the double-deck **Surb Astvatsatsin**, completed in 1339. It was designed as a memorial church. The ground floor contains the tombs of Prince Burtel and his family, and the first floor, linked by a narrow external staircase, acted as a chapel.

The western facade is particularly well decorated with exquisite original carvings. The tympanum on the lower doorway depicts the Holy Virgin with child, flanked by archangels; the upper tympanum shows Christ and Saints Peter and Paul. You can also see carved doves and sirens, and reliefs with geometric shapes and floral designs. The eastern facade presents a more simple appearance, although there are decorative elements such as columns, medallions and many crosses.

The **Surb Karapet** church was built in the 1220s by decree of Prince Liparit Orbelian and takes the usual plan of a cross within a square. A substantial gavit was added to the western side of the church in 1261, and inside this are many inscribed gravestones and khachkars. It is on the gavit's western facade where there are the most intricate surviving stone carvings. The tympanum over the door is semi-circular and shows the Holy Virgin sitting on a carpet. The carving is very detailed, right down to the tassels of the rug. Above the upper windows is a representation of God holding the head of John the Baptist.

The **Surb Grigor chapel** was added to the northern part of Surb Karapet church in 1275. It contains more Orbelian graves and of particular note is the carved stone of the Prince Tarsayich Orbelian's son. Dating from 1300, this shows an unusual lion-human hybrid figure.

Preparing for your visit to Yerevan

— Essential info —

When to visit

Yerevan has a continental-influenced climate, as it sits 900 m high on the Ararat Plain, surrounded by mountain ranges, and is remote from the sea. This geography results in long, hot, dry summers and relatively short, cold and snowy winters. Precipitation is relatively low, averaging only 12.5 inches during the year. Most of this falls in the spring and autumn, and the summer months of July and August are by far the driest.

Most seasons have their plus and minus points for visitors. Temperatures start to warm up in springs, with fresh greenery and flowers making a welcome appearance after the cold winter. However, this is the wettest period so bring an umbrella. Summers are drier. Temperatures in July and August can sometimes top 40 C in the middle of the day, although mornings and evenings remain pleasant. Autumn is the best time to visit. Temperatures are more moderate, and harvest time means delicious food. If you're a fan of winter sports, come in winter, as snow often lies on the ground for many weeks.

Visas

Armenia has a relaxed visa regime. Visitors from forty-five countries, including most of those in the EU, the United States, Australia, New Zealand, Japan and Singapore, can travel visa-free. A further seventy nationalities can apply for an e-visa online from the official Republic of Armenia e-Visa Issuance System, evisa.mfa.am. A visa for a short trip under twenty-one days currently costs USD 6. For all other nationalities, it is necessary to apply for a visa in advance at an Armenian embassy.

Currency

The currency is the Armenian Dram (AMD). Each Dram splits into 100 Luma. At the time of writing, May 2018, one US Dollar bought 485 Dram, one British Pound bought 660 Dram, and one Euro got 580 Dram. You can easily exchange these main currencies in the city, and exchanges and banks are commonplace. ATMs also accept Visa, Visa Electron, Mastercard and Maestro cards.

Time Zone

Yerevan is in the Armenia Time (AMT) zone, which is GMT+4. The country does not currently observe daylight savings time. As the city lies at the east of its time zone, summer evenings are agreeably light and long.

Electricity

Armenia's electricity is of the 220V/50Hz variety. The wall sockets take plugs with two round pins. Take a range of adaptors with you to make sure you can connect.

— Getting There and Away —

By Air

Yerevan's Zvartnots International Airport (IATA code EVN) is the primary international airport of Armenia and the busiest in the country. In the past few years, shiny new arrival and departure halls have been built, leading to the airport winning the 'Best Airport in the CIS' award in 2013.

Here are the airlines currently connecting **international destinations** with Yerevan:

- Aegean flies to Athens twice a week.
- Aeroflot has six flights every day to Moscow Sheremetyevo, with onward connections on its services and those of the SkyTeam Alliance. www.aeroflot.com
- Air Arabia links Yerevan with Sharjah four times each week. www.airarabia.com
- Air France flies to Paris Charles de Gaulle four times

weekly.

- Armenia Aircompany has multiple routes from Yerevan including Tel Aviv four times weekly and Beirut once a week. Mineralnye Vody, Voronezh, Cologne and Lyon are all served twice a week. www.armeniafly.com
- Atlas Global goes to Istanbul four times weekly.
- Austrian Airlines links Yerevan with Vienna five times each week.
- Belavia flies to Minsk, the Belorussian capital, twice a week.
- FlyDubai offers flights nine times a week to its Dubai hub, with onward connections around the Middle East, Africa, the Subcontinent, the Caucasus and Europe. www.flydubai.com. Alternatively, passengers can connect to Emirates' global network.
- Georgian Airways links Yerevan and Tbilisi six times a week.
- Iran Aseman www.iaa.ir and Mahan Air www.mahan.aero fly to Tehran, Iran.
- LOT links Yerevan to the Polish capital Warsaw daily. www.lot.com
- Middle East Airlines (MEA) has two flights a week to Beirut.
- Nordwind flies to Sochi twice a week and Moscow Sheremetyevo daily. www.nordwindairlines.ru
- Qatar Airways has daily flights to its hub at Doha, from where you can connect to its global network. www.qatarairways.com
- Redwings goes to Moscow Domedodovo daily. www.flyredwings.com
- S7 flies to Novosibirsk three times a week and Moscow Domodedovo three time daily. www.s7.ru
- SCAT has a weekly flight to Aktau, and a twice-

weekly service to Astana, both in Kazakhstan. www.scat.kz
- Turkmenistan Airlines flies to Ashgabat and Frankfurt once a week.
- Ukraine International Airlines flies to Kiev twelve times a week. www.flyuia.com
- Ural Airlines offers possibly the widest range of destinations from Yerevan, including daily flights to Moscow Domedodovo and Sochi. Other routes around Russia include Yekaterinberg, Krasnodar, Rostov on Don, Samara, and St Petersburg www.uralairlines.com
- UT Air has two services to Moscow Vnukovo on most days of the week.

As Armenia is a small country, there are no air services to other cities domestically.

By Rail

The Armenia railway network reaches into most parts of the country and comprises 845 km of track and around forty stations. In the face of the rapidly deteriorating railway and rolling stock, the Armenia government signed an agreement in 2008 transferring ownership to Russian Railways for thirty years. The network is now managed by their South Caucasus Railway division and is undergoing extensive modernisation.

The only international destination linked to Yerevan by rail is Tbilisi. Trains leave Tbilisi on the evening of every odd day of the month, with the journey taking ten hours. You arrive in Yerevan in time for breakfast. The return journey is similarly timed but on every even day. A seat will cost USD 20, and a sleeper USD 40, making this method of travel between the two cities the best value by far. Since the Nagorno-Karabakh war, services to Turkey, Azerbaijan and Iran remain suspended.

Domestically, daily services link Yerevan with Gyumri and Araks, both near the Turkish border, and with Yeraskh in the south. The fare is unlikely to exceed more than USD 15-20 anywhere in the country.

Tickets can be purchased online on the South Caucasus Railway website, www.ukzhd.am. The site also has full timetable and route information, displayed in English.

By Road

The most straightforward route is from Tbilisi in Georgia. You can find Mercedes Sprinter minibuses near the Avlabari metro station in the city centre. They leave throughout the day at two to three-hour intervals. A one-way ride to Yerevan will cost you about USD 15, and the journey will be for four to five hours, depending on the craziness of the driver. In the opposite direction, minibuses leave Yerevan from the Kilikia central bus station a little way to the southwest of the city centre.

It is also possible to travel from Yerevan to Tabriz in Iran. You can buy tickets at the Kikilikia bus station for around USD 55. The one daily bus leaves in the late morning and arrives in Tabriz in the very early hours of the next day. However, British, US and Canadian citizens should ensure that they comply with Iranian entry requirements, which generally necessitate being met by an official guide.

There are currently no open land crossings with Turkey and Azerbaijan.

By Boat

As Armenia is a landlocked country, there are no boat services. However, intrepid travellers journeying overland from Europe can take a boat to the Georgian cities of Batumi and Poti from Ukraine, and from there travel overland to Yerevan. An interesting alternative sea route is from Varna in Bulgaria to Poti, also in Georgia.

— Getting Around —

From the airport

Zvartnots International Airport is 12 km west of the city, almost as far as Vagharshapat. The quickest and most comfortable way to get to the centre of Yerevan is by taxi, and the one-way price for a taxi ride to most hotels is around 6000 AMD. Most taxis have a meter, and you should make sure that this works before you start off. The official airport taxi service is called AeroTaxi, and you can arrange a cab from their desk inside the arrivals hall.

A cheaper alternative is the newly-launched express bus service, which drops passengers at four points in Yerevan: Republic Square, Yeritasardakan Metro, the intersection of Abovyan and Say-Nova Streets, and the junction of Amiryan Street and Mashtots Avenue. Buses leave every half an hour between 7 am and 10 pm, and hourly during the night. The one-way fare is only 300 AMD. To find the bus, look out for the signs in the arrivals hall. On the journey back to the airport, the bus picks up at the same drop-off points.

The Yerevan metro system does not currently stretch as far as the airport.

Around the city

As explained in the detailed walking tours in this guide, the majority of sights are accessible on foot. However, for when feet get tired, or if the weather is not cooperating, there are some public transport options.

The Yerevan Metro has a single line that runs north-south through the central district, with a total length of 14 km. While most stations in the suburbs will be of little interest to visiting tourists, the central portion of the track provides a quick way of getting around Kentron. This runs from Zoravar Andanik station near Saint Gregory the Illuminator cathedral to Republic Square and then on to Yeritasardakan station near Freedom Square and Matenadaran. A trip anywhere on the metro system costs 100 AMD; you will need to buy a plastic token which you then put in the turnstile to access the station.

The most popular way for locals to get around the city is by one of the ubiquitous twelve or sixteen-seater minibuses, or marshrutka. More than one hundred routes crisscross the city. The minibuses prominently display the service number on the front windscreen, and you can hail them from various points along their fixed routes. Journeys cost 100 AMD, and you pay the driver when you get off. It is best to avoid marshrutkas in the rush hours when overcrowding can become quite extreme.

Taxis can be hailed easily from anywhere in central districts. You should be able to get to any destination within Kentron for around 1000 AMD. Many companies operate around the city, and all their cars should have a taxi sign on the roof and yellow number plates. Make sure that the meter is working before starting any journey. Companies include Prestige, Rich, Pink, Niu Pogodi, Elegant, Just, and Ani Plus, and instead of hailing a cab you can ring their call centres to order one. For the ultimate convenience, try GG Taxi, whose cars can be ordered online using their app, downloadable from the AppStore and Google Play.

— Where to stay —

Yerevan has a good supply of reasonably priced accommodation, even in peak months such as August. There are also many Airbnb (www.airbnb.com) options available, although you have to be careful that these are not too far out in the suburbs. Here are just a few highlights in the top end and mid-range categories, however www.booking.com lists all the possible options at the competitive rates. Furthermore, Tripadvisor.com compares prices with the three or four top hotel consolidators, making sure you get the most reasonable rate.

Top end

Yerevan Marriott is located right on Republic Square, so its location is impossible to beat. The hotel offers luxurious rooms, multiple dining options, gym, and an outdoor pool which is a rarity in central Yerevan.

Hyatt Place Yerevan is a fantastic, casual and contemporary property, located on a quiet side street just off the Republic Square. It has a superb location steps from some of Yerevan's major sights. All guests can enjoy a free hot breakfast buffet each morning, and there is an on-site gym.

Royal Tulip Grand Hotel Yerevan is an elegant luxury option, housed in a 1920s neoclassical building. It fronts Charles Aznavour Square, in the midst of an area famed for its shopping and nightlife. The hotel boasts a rooftop swimming pool which opens each summer season.

DoubleTree by Hilton Yerevan City Centre is situated a few steps from English Park and about a ten-minute walk from Republic Square. This good-value hotel offers modern guest rooms, a spa, gym, outdoor bar and complimentary hot breakfast buffet.

Tufenkian Historic Yerevan Hotel faces the Vernissage Market in the heart of the city. Beautifully designed throughout, this recent addition to the Yerevan hotel scene is the result of a collaboration between Armenian designers and globally-renowned architects.

Mid-range

Ibis Yerevan Centre is a brand-new hotel centrally-located between the Northern Avenue and Abovyan Street shopping districts. With its comfortable guest rooms, restaurant, 24/7 bar and free wifi, it's a great option.

Nova Hotel on Sayat-Nova Street is cosy boutique hotel a short walk from either Republic or Freedom Squares. It offers multiple room categories, including studio suite with kitchenette, all coming with free wifi.

Capitals of the Caucasus

* * *

Paris Hotel is located in downtown a two-minute walk from Republic Square and markets itself as offering some of the biggest beds in Yerevan. The hotel has a roof-top cafe-bar with panoramic views over the city towards Mount Ararat.

Republica Hotel is highly-rated online and is within walking distance of all the sites. The guest rooms are a unique blend of all the modern facilities you'd expect, with a traditional feel expressed through the use of old Armenian carpet designs.

My Hotel Yerevan is a new micro-boutique hotel located just the other side of Circular Park from the downtown area. It has twelve luxury bedrooms and complimentary breakfast and wifi.

BAKU | *Azerbaijan*

The largest and most dynamic city in the Caucasus, Baku is often overlooked by visitors in favour of its neighbours Tbilisi and Yerevan. Yet it is far and away the most exciting destination in the region, and deserves to be high up on any history-lover's bucket list. The city is booming, and while some liken it to its brash Middle Eastern cousin, Dubai, it offers much more than just glittering skyscrapers and marble-clad shopping centres. Baku has witnessed almost two millennia of tumultuous history and has been witness to the rise and fall of a succession of empires, and this has left its mark on the city you see today.

Baku's beautifully-preserved old town harbours ancient mosques, palaces, towers, caravanserais and hammams within the confines of imposing twelfth-century defensive walls. The city has been home over time to Zoroastrians, Arabs, Ottomans, Persians, Shirvants and Russians, and each has left their indelible mark. Spreading out from the shores of the Caspian Sea, leafy boulevards lined with oil boom-era mansions give the feel of a European capital, with glitzy boutiques and Mercedes aplenty. Elsewhere, grey Soviet-era apartment blocks jostle for space with a Zaha Hadid-designed architectural masterpiece. Rusting railway tracks and nodding donkey oil wells encircle a centuries-old

Zoroastrian fire temple. Hillsides burn and mud volcanoes bubbles. Baku is all this and much more; a vibrant mix of heady flavours, from different cultures, religion and periods. Only by diving deep into its treasures can you truly appreciate it.

The good news is that now is the perfect time to visit. Baku offers a modern, traveller-friendly infrastructure, with a wide selection of hotels and restaurants catering to every taste. Public transport stretches into every corner of the city, making it easy and cost-effective to see all the sights. And what's even better, the visa regime has been significantly relaxed, with many nationalities eligible to apply for e-visas. So now's the time to visit, and this book will be your companion as you explore the city. Welcome to Baku.

Contents

- *Getting to know Baku* gives a brief history of the city and examines its history, geography and demographics.
- *Baku Walking Tour 1* takes you on a walking tour around the main sights of Baku's old city.
- *Baku Walking Tour 2* explores the nineteenth century oil baron mansions in the boom town.
- *Baku Walking Tour 3* visits the stunning parks perched on the highest slopes of Baku.
- *Baku Walking Tour 4* takes a stroll along the beautiful corniche running next to the Caspian Sea and then indulges in some retail therapy.
- *Day Trips from Baku* takes in the sights of the city suburbs and further afield.
- *Preparing for your visit* gives you all the essential practical information needed to make your trip plain sailing.

List of Maps

- **Map A**: Double Gates to Maiden tower

- **Map B**: Maiden Tower to the Palace of the Shirvanshahs
- **Map C**: Palace of the Shirvanshahs
- **Map D**: Palace of the Shirvanshahs back to the Double Gates
- **Map E**: Boom Town
- **Map F**: Parks and Panoramas
- **Map G**: Carpet Museum and along Baku Boulevard
- **Map H**: Baku Boulevard to Fountain Square
- **Map I**: Ateshgah Fire Temple
- **Map J**: Yanar Dag
- **Map K**: Heydar Aliyev Centre
- **Map L**: Gobustan National Park

Getting to know Baku

A brief history

A hundred thousand years ago, the semi-arid land around modern-day Baku was instead grassy savanna with a wealth of animal and plant life. It is natural that humans would have been present to some extent, and indeed some traces of habitation have been found from the Stone Age. Moving forward into the Bronze age, the evidence that there was a settlement where Baku now sits grows stronger and includes rock carvings in the area now home to Baku's Bayil suburb, and an astronomical observatory in Nardarn to the city's north. In the first century AD, the Romans reached this part of the world, and today's village of Ramana appears on their maps. There is a shortage of information about the Baku area during the following centuries, although the fifth-century Greek historian Priscus did mention the "Bakuvian fires" emanating from the ground.

The region eventually became known as Shirvan, and from the mid-ninth century was ruled by the Shirvanshahs (literally "Kings of Shirvan"). They were destined to reign until the sixteenth century, although during this time

Shirvan's independence was punctuated by long periods of subordination by other neighbouring powers, reducing it to a vassal state.

The twelfth century was a period of relative stability, and the Shirvanshahs were able to set about building strong defences, including the fortifications surrounding the old city of Baku and the Maiden Tower, to resist their many foreign enemies. Nevertheless, Baku and Shirvan were overrun by the Mongols in 1235, which ushered in two brutal centuries of Mongol, and then Timurid, subordination.

The fortunes of the Shirvan state were revived in the fifteenth century when Shirvanshah Ibrahim I succeeded in repelling the foreign oppressors. Together with his successors, Khalilullah I and Farrukh Yassar, the Shirvanshahs then oversaw a period of renaissance, during which the Palace of the Shirvanshahs was built. However, this was not to last, and in 1501 Shirvan and Baku was invaded by Safavid King Ismail I, whose forces ransacked the city and even exhumed the bodies from the Shirvanshah mausoleum. While Shirvan managed to limp along as a vassal state for a few more years, Ismail I's son, Tahmasp I, fully incorporated it into the Safavid empire in 1538, putting an end once and for all to the Shirvanshah reign.

Safavid rule lasted for the next two centuries until 1722 when Russian and Ottoman forces invaded Baku. For the rest of the eighteenth century, this heralded varying degrees of Russian influence, Shirvan independence and conflicts between Russian and Persian armies. At the very end of the century, Russia began a concerted effort to conquer the Caucasus once and for all, and Baku was captured and fully integrated into the Russian Empire by 1813.

In 1846 the world's first oil well was drilled in the Bibi-Heybat suburb of Baku, marking the start of the oil boom. A period of frenzied development followed for the rest of the nineteenth century, and well into the twentieth, which saw the city rapidly expand from its old core. Many palatial mansions, civic amenities, parks and boulevards were built during this time by magnates such as Musa Naigiyev, Murtuza Mukhtarov and Shamsi Asadullayev. By World War I, Baku was producing 15% of the entire world's oil output.

After the collapse of the Russian Empire in 1918, independence was declared and the short-lived "Azerbaijan Democratic Republic" was founded. However, in April 1920 the Russian Red Army crossed the border, captured Baku the next day, and went on to occupy the whole country. The city then became the capital of the "Azerbaijan Soviet Socialist Republic".

The wait to become independent again was to last for more than seventy years. In 1991, following the collapse of the USSR, the Azerbaijani flag flew once more over a free country. Baku has now become the vibrant beating heart of Azerbaijan, and the centre for science, culture, politics and industry.

Geography

Baku is Azerbaijan's capital and the largest city in the Caucasus. It is situated in the extreme east of Azerbaijan on the Absheron peninsula, which juts out into the waters of the Caspian Sea, and lies just above 40 degrees north. A surprising geographical anomaly is that much of Baku sits well under sea level, at -28 m, making it the world's lowest capital city. Its more famous counterpart, Amsterdam, is a mere 2 m below sea level.

Like the pearl in an oyster, the heart of the city is the compact old town or "Icherisheher" in Azerbaijani. Inside its ancient walls, the streets are narrow and winding and there is a merciful absence of traffic. Spreading out from the old town away from the sea is a band of development created during the nineteenth-century oil boom when money flooded in and Baku outgrew the confines of the old city walls. This area has broad boulevards, leafy parks and lavish mansions. Spreading out once more from this "Boom Town" is the modern-day city which started to grow up during Soviet times, with roads laid out on a more rigid grid pattern. The outlying suburbs are home to heavy industry, oil extraction and quarries.

Leading the city's main thoroughfares is the ever-busy Neftchilar Prospect which runs parallel to the Caspian Sea shoreline. The road begins at Baku Crystal Hall in the south, runs past the old city and Government House, before changing its name to Nobel Prospect and heading out across the Absheron Peninsula. Azadliq Prospect runs north across the entire city from Government House, past 28 May Station and beyond. Finally, from Nizami Park, near the Double Gates of the Old Town, the Zerbaycan Prospect eventually passes the bus station and 20 January metro before splitting into the M1 and M4 national motorways.

Demographics

Just over 2.3 million people live in Baku, which means that a quarter of the entire Azerbaijan population lives within its municipal limits. While in Soviet times there were sizeable Russian and Armenian populations, Baku today is less cosmopolitan with the city comprising more than 90% native Azerbaijanis.

The majority of people follow Shia Islam. However, Azerbaijan is a secular state and conserves religious freedom. Accordingly, you can find synagogues and a wide variety of churches serving Christian minorities.

Languages

Azerbaijani is the official language, a Turkic language closely related and partially mutually intelligible with modern day Turkish. It is the native tongue of 92.5% of Azerbaijanis. Half of the population is monolingual, and among those speaking other languages, English and Russian are the most popular. In the Nagorno-Karabakh enclave Armenian is spoken, although this area is not under government control.

Baku Walking Tour 1 - Old Town (Icherisheher)

All of Baku used to be contained with the walls of the present-day old town, and it was only in the mid-nineteenth century, with the advent of the oil industry, that the city eventually expanded beyond the walls and then kept on growing. It was at this time that the area within the walls became aptly known as "Icherisheher", which is Azerbaijani for "Inner City".

Icherisheher was built in the middle ages, and the twelfth century saw the erection of the Maiden Tower and a surge in construction within the city walls. The old town comprised a maze of winding streets, which can still be seen today, dividing it into nine separate districts. These neighbourhoods were centred on a mosque, many of which still stand such as the Juma, Siniqqala, Mohammed and Shah mosques, each with a mullah.

Every merchant and artisan had a shop and many of these clustered together in a great bazaar stretching from Juma mosque to the Maiden Tower. Buyers and suppliers came from all over Azerbaijan, and from Persia, Russia and Central Asia. To cater to the needs of all these visitors, and residents, many lavish caravanserais and bathhouses were built. Then in the relative stability of the fifteenth-century, the

Shirvanshah rulers built their palace on high ground overlooking the entire city.

Many of these mosques, caravanserais, bathhouses, bazaars, walls and towers are well preserved, making Icherisheher a living history book. This walking tour, split into manageable chunks, takes in all the highlights.

— Double Gates to Maiden Tower —

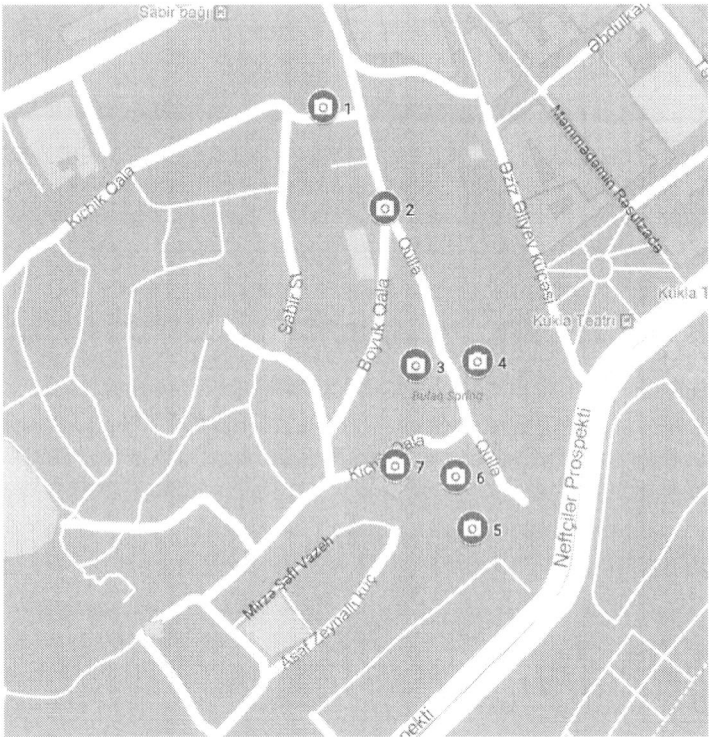

Map A | Double Gates to Maiden Tower
* * *

Double Gate (Qosa Qala Qapisi)

Construction of Baku's old city walls started as far back as the twelfth century. A plaque in Arabic script was uncovered during restoration work, detailing that the wall was '… ordered by the glorious, wise, just, victorious, ruling monarch, supporter of Islam and of Muslims, the great Shirvanshah Abdul Khoja Manujohr.' This ruler was on the throne from 1120 to 1149, nicely pinpointing the construction date.

Today, 500 m of Baku's old city walls remain standing, and the most impressive feature of this stretch of monumental masonry is the Double Gate, or Qosa Qala Qapisi *(Map A, Point 1)*. This portal connects the ancient city with the more recent nineteenth-century neighbourhood built during the oil boom years.

In bas-relief above each of the gates is the ancient coat of arms of Baku, showing two lions either side of a bull's head, along with a representation of the sun and moon. In the seventeenth century, the German explorer Kaempfer tried to decipher the meaning of this coat of arms with local historians. He determined that the bull represents the city of Baku itself, as in ancient times the land could not adequately support crops and locals turned to cattle farming instead. The flanking lions protect the bull, or city, and so represent the walls themselves. The moon and sun show that this protection is unwavering, and continues both during the day and at night.

Museum of Archaeology and Ethnography

Once you have passed through the Double Gates, you are in

the Old Town proper. Walking straight down the cobbled street, you will see many buildings with the distinctive architectural feature of balconies hanging over the road. Carpet sellers are everywhere. Eventually, the road forks and the Museum of Ethnography and Archaeology *(Map A, Point 2)* is located at this junction.

The archaeological display at the museum covers Azerbaijani history from the Stone Age through to the Middle Ages. Artefacts show how these early people lived, and sheds light on their art, lifestyle, culture and values. The focus of the ethnographic section is on more recent times and looks at life during the nineteenth and twentieth centuries.

The museum is open weekdays between 10 am and 5 pm. It is closed on Saturdays and Sundays.

Caravanserais

Back at the junction outside the museum, take the left-hand fork. This narrow street leads to two facing caravanserais. These provided weary travellers with accommodation, and also somewhere to eat, feed their horses, camels and mules, hire temporary guards and meet new trading partners. All caravanserais are designed for safety and security; any potential assailants are hindered by just one entrance and windows only facing the interior courtyard.

On the right-hand side of the street is the fifteenth-century Bukhara Caravanserai *(Map A, Point 3)*, so called because traders from modern-day Uzbekistan built it. Initially used by Central Asian merchants, this square building has cells arrayed along each wall, facing inwards into a calm, octagonal courtyard.

On the left, the fourteenth-century Multani Caravanserai *(Map A, Point 4)* takes its name from the Pakistani city

Multan, established by visitors and merchants from the subcontinent. These were possibly the same people involved in the development of the Ateshgah Fire Temple. This caravanserai has a similar construction to the one just across the street. Today, both are fancy restaurants, offering a wide range of Azerbaijani cuisine.

Approaching Maiden Tower

A few steps from the caravanserais will take you out into an open area, behind which the Maiden Tower *(Map A, Point 5)* looms. The area below street level is the excavated remains of a seventeenth-century marketplace *(Map A, Point 6)*. It comprises a large inner courtyard surrounded by an iwan, which is a vaulted, rectangular construction open on one side. In the market are displays of tombstones, sarcophagi and carvings that were found in Baku and across the Absheron peninsula.

Next to the marketplace is the distinctive dome-roofed Hadji Bani bathhouse *(Map A, Point 7)*, built in the late fifteenth-century. The bathhouse had remained undiscovered until archaeological excavations in the 1960s. Although today we think of bathing as a fundamentally private activity to be conducted in the sanctuary of our bathroom, in the Middle Ages they played a vital public role. They promoted health and hygiene and were also a place where people could go to relax and unwind. The Old Town of Baku has many bathhouses, often situated close to caravanserais. After a long, tiring journey along one of the many Silk Roads, the bathhouse represented a very welcome luxury, and one not to be missed.

* * *

— Maiden Tower (Qiz Qalasi) —

The imposing and ancient Maiden Tower looms over the Old Town and is the iconic landmark of Baku. While Paris has the Eiffel Tower and London Big Ben, this structure represents Baku. Maiden Tower became a UNESCO World Heritage Site due to its historical significance, and today graces the 10 Manat banknote and 5 Gepik coin.

The tower is a cylinder, just shy of 30 m high and with a diameter of 16.5 m. Inside there are eight floors, linked by a winding stone staircase. A buttress, the same height of the tower, sticks out of the tower on the seaward side. The solidity of construction is staggering, and the tower is built on a massive slab of rock, with foundations extending down 14 m. The walls at the base are 5 m thick and contain an ingenious drainage system designed to carry sewerage and wastewater from each of the floors.

These are all concrete facts. So far so good. But now the confusion begins. There are many conflicting theories regarding the history of the tower, its purpose, its date of construction and just about everything else. To borrow a quote from Winston Churchill, the tower is "a riddle, wrapped in a mystery, inside an enigma".

An impressive museum is arranged over the internal floors, with each level examining the conflicting theories and attempting to peel back some of these layers of mystery. As you climb upwards you will eventually reach the flat roof of the tower, from where you get a 360-degree panoramic view of Baku's Old Town, Boom Town, Flame Towers, Corniche and the glittering Caspian Sea.

There have been a few reconstructions of the tower in the past decades. During the most recent of these, from 2009-13, the stone walls were extensively renovated. Interestingly, the nooks and crannies between these stones were home to common swifts. The archaeologists did not want to make these birds homeless, so they built small replacement nests on the walls of the neighbouring buildings. So when wandering around the area of the tower, keep your eyes open, and you may see some of the swifts flying in and out of their new homes!

Theories abound

There are no surviving written sources which document the construction or purpose of the tower and, accordingly, scientists, architects, historians and academics have come up with a mind-boggling range of theories. However, these theories coalesce into four primary schools of thought.

The first of these theoretical conclusions is that the tower was a Zoroastrian temple dedicated to ancient pre-Islamic Persian goddesses Mitra and Anahita. In the mid-1980s, local Azeri researchers Davud Akhundov and Hassan Hassanov found archaeological evidence showing that there were purportedly seven fire exits on the top of the structure. Supporting this theory of religious and ritual use is the shape of the tower when seen from above. It resembles a teardrop, or number 6 or 9, depending on one's viewpoint. This shape is known as the buta, a symbol of the fire and light that is important in Zoroastrianism. The Paisley pattern so familiar in modern-day clothing design derives from the buta, and this motif is found in many other artistic applications in old Baku. Today, fires still burn on the roof during the Persian new year Nowruz celebrations, a festival which has strong links to Zoroastrianism.

Other scholars believe that the tower had a more practical defensive purpose. A secret tunnel linking the Palace of the Shirvanshahs to the Maiden Tower lends credence to this theory, as does the integral well in the centre of the structure which would allow people within the tower to get fresh water while under siege. However, academics supporting the defence-related theory divide into two camps of thought. The first set of scholars believe that the tower dates to around the twelfth century, the same time the Old Town's defensive walls were built. The second group put forward the theory that the tower was built as a stand-alone structure much earlier in the fifth or sixth century. They have identified similarities with other similarly-aged castles and towers part of the northern Persian empire defensive network. They also point to differences in the stone used to construct the tower than that used in the adjacent city walls.

A final theory states that the tower was an astronomical observatory. An Azeri archaeologist, Gara Ahmadov, claims that the thirty stone projections on the bottom part of the tower, and a further thrity-one stone markers on the upper part, are related to the days of the month. While this opinion is widely discredited, there is still little evidence to support the other theories, and so cannot be wholly ruled out.

Legends

Many legends swirl around the tower, as you'd expect for something that has stood so prominently in Baku for well over a thousand years. The most widely told legend is that of a king who fell in love with his daughter and decided to marry her. Understandably the daughter did not particularly welcome this prospect, so she attempted to delay the marriage by asking her father to build the loftiest tower possible. His passion was such that he did just that, and the result was the tower you see today. The daughter then climbed the stairs, telling her father she was going to admire the view, but instead threw herself off and crashed onto the rocks far below. This tale, in many varying forms, is still told in Azeris plays and poetry. The national ballet troupe even performs it, and while in Baku you may be lucky enough to see it staged.

So according to this legend the name Maiden Tower makes sense. However, as with everything else concerning this structure, there are differences of opinion regarding its nomenclature. Some believe 'maiden' refers to the towers' impregnability. Others think that maiden, 'qiz' in Azerbaijani, refers to the water goddess Anahita that features in the Avesta, the Zoroastrian holy book. Whatever the truth, the Maiden Tower does not look likely to reveal any of its secrets any time soon.

— Maiden Tower to the Palace of the Shirvanshahs —

* * *

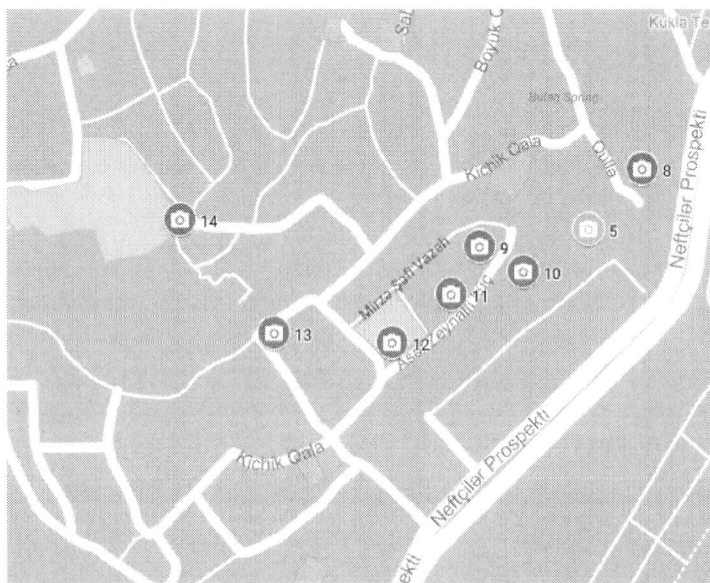

Map B | Maiden Tower to the Palace of the Shirvanshahs

Before you set off for the other jewel of the Old Town, the Palace of the Shirvanshahs, take a moment to walk around to the side of the Maiden Tower that faces the Caspian Sea. As you look at the tower, you will see an ornate building to its right. This is the Hajinski Mansion *(Map B, Point 8)*.

Hajinski Mansion

This prominent neighbour of the Maiden Tower was built in 1912 for the wealthy local oil baron Isa Bey Hajinski, and was at that time one of the tallest buildings in the city. There are many art nouveau flourishes, comic faces carved into the limestone of the building, and mosaics in the style of ancient Assyria. Seven individually-design spires and balconies in a variety of styles adorn this majestic building. The building's aim was to communicate the power and status of its owner, and it undoubtedly achieves this goal.

However, there is a distinct lack of harmony between the various building facades. As an explanation, it is alleged that the architect funnelled funds materials into the construction of his own lavish house, although there are indications that this was standard practice during this period.

Hajinski died in 1918, just after the Russian revolution. During the Soviet time, the building was split up into different apartments, often used by visiting dignitaries, the most famous of whom was General Charles de Gaulle in 1944. Another celebrated resident was Yusif Mammadaliyev, an outstanding Azerbaijani chemist and twice President of the National Academy of Sciences.

In 2007 the facades of the building were comprehensively renovated. Nowadays the ground floor is home to the stores of exclusive brands, such as Tiffany, Bvlgari and Christian Dior.

Go back up towards the other side of Maiden tower. Turn left, and you will be at the beginning of Asaf Zeynalli Street. This thoroughfare takes its name from the accomplished Azerbaijani composer, who wrote many symphonies and folk songs before his untimely death aged 23. The leading music school of Azerbaijan is also named after him.

Along this street are many buildings of note.

Madrasa Mosque

Diagonally across the plaza fronting the Maiden Tower is the tiny Madrasa Mosque *(Map B, Point 9)*, dating to the twelfth century. Its shape is an almost perfect cube topped out with a small dome, and has no minarets. The name 'Madrasa' derives from the Arabic word for school, and in this building mullahs taught students the Qur'an, natural sciences, mathematics and eastern languages, and also trained aspiring secondary school teachers.

These days the building is inhabited by carpet and souvenir sellers.

Mugham Club

Opposite the Madrasa Mosque is the Mugam Club *(Map B, Point 10)*, a restaurant housed in an old and picturesque caravanserai. Its two-storey wings enclose a pleasant courtyard containing tables interspersed with small trees and fountains. If you're passing by at lunch or dinner time, it's a great place to try out some Azerbaijani food, and in the evening there are traditional music and dance performances.

Ashur (Lezgi) Mosque

A few steps down A. Zeynalli Street, on the right-hand side, is the Ashur Mosque *(Map B, Point 11)*, which takes its name from the twelfth-century architect Najaf Ashur Ibrahim. In the nineteenth century, the mosque became known informally as the Lezgi mosque. During that time many men from Dagestan, Russia, came to Baku to work in the oil boom. These were mostly of the Lezgin ethnic group, and as they prayed mainly at this mosque, the name entered public etymology. Inside there is a single prayer hall.

The shape of the mosque is parallelepiped, or in other words a slightly elongated cube. Some academics believe that this twelfth-century building sits over a much earlier fire-worshipping temple. Archaeological investigations are still ongoing, and in the future yet more of this site's long history may be unearthed.

Juma (Friday) Mosque

A short distance further down A. Zeynalli Street, on the same side, is the Juma, or Friday, Mosque *(Map B, Point 12)*. The entrance to the mosque is a beautifully and intricately carved portal, replete with geometric and floral designs and Arabic calligraphy. This site has had a long and eventful history, and as with the Ashur mosque, archaeologists suggest that the Juma mosque was originally built over a Zoroastrian fire-worshipping temple in the twelfth century. The minaret, built in 1437 by Shirvan Shah Khalilullah I, is decorated with elaborate stalactite carvings (muqarnas), a common architectural feature found in mosques across Iran. The mosque itself has been rebuilt several times over the centuries, and the philanthropy of the merchant Haji Shikhladi Dadashov in 1899 paid for the construction of the present structure.

Inside, four stout columns in the square prayer hall support a single dome covered in ornate tilework reminiscent of that found in noteworthy Persian buildings in modern-day Iran.

Mohammed Mosque

Turn right after the Juma Mosque, and at the end of the street turn left. After a few steps, you will see the imposing bulk of the minaret of the Muhammed Mosque *(Map B, Point 13)*, one of the oldest buildings in the whole of the Old Town, built in 1078-1079.

The mosque also goes by the name Synyk Gala, roughly translated as 'damaged tower'. This second name came about during the Russo-Persian War in the eighteenth century. Russian warships bombarded Baku, and a shell hit the minaret. Soon after, a storm blew the ships far out to sea, and the inhabitants of Baku took this as a sign of divine retribution. The damaged minaret was eventually repaired in the mid-nineteenth century.

Retrace your steps back along the road outside the mosque, and go straight. Then take the first left and walk uphill. After a meandering 200 m or so you will reach the back of the Palace of the Shirvanshahs. Located on this back wall is the magnificent Murad's Gate *(Map B, Point 14)*.

Murad's Gate

The gate was built much later than the rest of the palace in 1585. At this time, the Ottomans were at war with the neighbouring Safavid Persian Empire, and as part of this campaign, the Turks captured Baku. Accordingly, the gate was named to honour the victorious Sultan of the Ottoman Empire, Murad III.

A celebrated Persian architect from Tabriz designed the gate. The uppermost part of the gate has an Arabic inscription, which states that 'this noble building was built in the days of rule of the most just and the greatest sultan Murad Ulu Rajab-baba Bakuji in the year 994 (1585). Either side of this are two roundels with floral motifs. The semi-dome recess has the stalactites, or muqarnas, popular in Persian architecture at this time. As the gate is much wider than other entrances, this could have been a portal into a building that was either subsequently demolished or not built at all.

From Murad's Gate, walk along the road that follows the palace walls. Eventually, you will emerge at the front entrance of the palace. The ticket office is here.

— Palace of the Shirvanshahs —

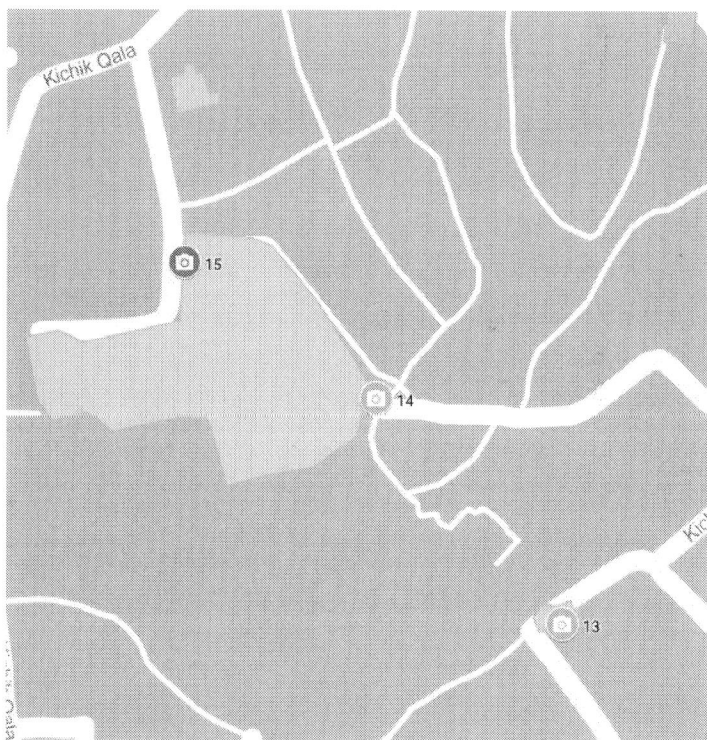

Map C | Palace of the Shirvanshahs

The Palace of the Shirvanshahs *(Map C, Point 15)* is undoubtedly one of the two gems of Baku, the other being the Maiden Tower, and a visit here should be on the top of every visitor's list. Shah Khalilullah I began construction in the early fifteenth century when he moved the capital of the Shirvan state from Shamakhy to Baku. The name Shirvanshahs translates into English as 'Kings of the Shirvan'. The complex is now regarded as being the finest example of Shirvan architecture and is designated a UNESCO World Heritage Site. It's importance to the nation is undeniable, and graces the back of the 10 Manat banknote.

The entire palace complex is at one of the highest points of the old city, and there are far-reaching views from many places. When first built, the palace was integrated with the surrounding city, and the high walls were only added in the nineteenth century.

Due to the local topography, the various buildings are arrayed on three different levels. Fronting the highest courtyard is the main palace building itself and the Divankhana. In the intermediary yard are the Seyid Yahya Mausoleum, Keygubad Mosque and the Baiolv Stones. Slightly lower again is the Palace Mosque and Family Mausoleum. At the very lowest level is the Hammam.

Eighteenth-century naval bombardments severely damaged the palace, and restoration work has been ongoing since then.

The Upper Courtyard

Once past the ticket counter, you enter the upper courtyard, bordered on three sides by palace buildings with the fourth offering expansive views over Baku towards the Flame Towers. As you walk towards the entrance to the Palace building, you will notice many dozens of bullet holes peppering the stone walls, visible reminders of the Armenian-Azeri conflict of 1918.

Main palace building

The palace itself dates back to the early fifteenth century, 1411 to be precise, and its construction was ordered by Shirvanshah Sheyyk Ibrahim I. It has a total of 52 rooms arrayed over two floors connected by three narrow winding stairways. The King and the royal family used the upper part, and so the steps in the main arched entranceway go all the way up to that floor. The lower level was for servants and household staff.

One of the most impressive rooms is the Throne Hall, which acted as a focal point for palace life and state events. An idea of its previous glory is given by the fifteenth-century court poet, Badr Shirvani, who wrote: "It is blue as the sky and golden as the sun here. When light passes through the windows to fall upon the ceiling full of decorative designs, the stars shine from within the blue glow of the dome". Indeed, archaeologists have found evidence that blue tiles adorned the interior of the palace. Another highlight is the Banquet Hall, and you should look out for the windows covered in geometric stone latticework, through which you can glimpse lovely views of the Caspian Sea.

Today, artefacts and relics from throughout the palace's long history are displayed in many of the palace rooms. However, due to looting and bombardments during the sixteenth to eighteenth centuries by Russian and Ottoman forces, most items on display are from the last two hundred years or so. Nonetheless, there are many fascinating and beautiful artefacts from swords, musical instruments and clothing through to household objects, carpets and jewellery.

Divankhana

Back out in the upper courtyard, walk through a small doorway in the northern wall to see the Divankhana, regarded as the most exceptional examples of medieval architecture anywhere in the Middle East.

The Divankhana is a small octagonal pavilion, surrounded by an open balcony edged with columns and arches, on a raised platform. This construction is in the centre of a courtyard surrounded by a gallery-arcade with similarly-shaped columns and arches.

The main entrance is particularly ornate. There are striking floral motifs representing fig and vine leaves, plants common throughout Azerbaijan. Stalactites or muqarnas support a fluted semi-cupola. Either side of the entrance are two hexagonal inscriptions, the left reading "There is no God but Allah" and "Prophet Mohammed is the messenger of Allah", and the right repeating "Allah is single" and "Mohammed" six times each. Once you walk through this portal, you enter a vestibule with yet more floral carvings and Arabic calligraphy, before reaching the pavilion itself.

There is still much debate regarding the use of this building. Some scholars believe that it was a royal courthouse, others think that it was used for receiving visiting delegations, while yet more see evidence that it was a royal tomb for Farrukh Yassar.

Walk back into the upper courtyard, and walk straight across to find the staircase leading to the middle and lower courtyards.

The Middle Courtyard

The Mausoleum of Seyid Yahya

Seyid Yahya was a royal scholar and astronomer in the court of Khalilullah I. His mausoleum is situated in a separate, slightly sunken courtyard, and is octagonally-shaped with a distinctive 7.5 m high pyramidal roof. It resembles tombs found in the medieval Seljuk Turko-Persian empire.

The mausoleum comprises a lower subterranean part containing the tomb itself, and an upper portion used for religious ceremonies. The building is attached to the oldest part of the palace, the Keygubad Mosque, which is now in ruins.

The Bailov Stones

Displayed around the external walls of the middle courtyard are the thirteenth-century Bailov Stones. All these come from Sabayil Fortress, which was built on a small island 300 m out in the Caspian Sea.

This fortress was a substantial structure, more than 175 m long and 35 m wide, with two-metre thick walls, three circular and twelve semi-circular towers. A scale model in one of the rooms of the main palace building shows the Sabayil Fortress as it would have been in its prime.

However, the building did not last long. In 1306 there was a cataclysmic earthquake in the Caspian Sea which not only caused the castle to crumble but also led to the sea level dramatically rising. The ruins were submerged, in effect becoming Azerbaijan's very own Atlantis, which was not rediscovered until the eighteenth century when water levels dropped again. Today you can still see its outline from the top of the Maiden Tower.

In 1939, an archaeological expedition found more than 700 inscribed stones, some of which now reside in this courtyard. These formed a frieze that completely encircled the castle walls. Humans and animals such as horses and camels embellish the letters on these stones, and it is rare to see such examples of Arabic inscriptions in an anthropomorphic style. Historians analysing them have found the names of fifteen individual Shirvanshahs and other valuable historical information from that time.

The Lower Courtyard

A wall separates the lower courtyard from the other sections of the palace. Here there are two buildings, the Palace Mosque and the Shirvanshah's Mausoleum.

Palace Mosque

This mosque was built in the mid-fifteenth century, and an inscription around the 22 m high minaret confirms this, stating that "The Great Sultan Khalilullah I order the erection of this minaret. May God preserve his rule as Shah. Year 845". That year in the Islamic calendar corresponds to 1441-42 in the Gregorian calendar.

The central part of the mosque consists of a square domed prayer hall, with a smaller adjacent hall for women. Upon entry, you can see the Mihrab on the facing wall, which indicates the direction of Mecca and acts as a kind of doorway to the holy city. In the upper corners of the mosque, and around the lower part of the dome, the necks of large jars protrude from the stonework. These were added to enhance the acoustics of the prayer hall.

* * *

The Mausoleum of the Shirvanshahs

The royal family's mausoleum is a rectangular-shaped building topped with an octagonal dome decorated with stars. Many years ago, these stars would have been filled in with blue tiles. The grand entrance to the building has many of the features seen in other portals in the palace, including floral carvings, stalactites and a concave semi-cupola. The inscription above the door indicates the purpose of the building, saying that "Khalilullah I...ordered to construct this light burial vault for his mother and son in 839" (1435-36). The two tear-drop shaped inscriptions either side of the portal show the architect's name, Memar Ali, along with the words God and Mohammed.

The court poet, Badr Shirvani, again helps us to shed some light on the use of the mausoleum. He recorded that the tomb houses the graces of Khalilullah I himself, his mother, four sons, a cousin and the army commander.

The mausoleum has had a violent past, however, and it was not the peaceful resting place as initially intended. In 1500, the Safavids invaded Baku, and they went about vandalising all of the graves in the mausoleum. It eventually turned out that it was only the tombstones that were destroyed, and the graves underneath escaped without damage.

The Lowest Courtyard

Excavations of the former palace bathhouse

The remains of the seventeenth-century palace bathhouse are on the lowest level of the royal complex and were only discovered in 1939. This hammam was built almost entirely underground to preserve warmth in the winter and to keep it cool in summer months, and only the cupolas poked above ground. The complex had a total of 26 rooms, and the king had his own personal bathroom.

The water came from a reservoir located behind the palace walls, and was heated in a boiler room and then distributed throughout the bathing rooms. Steam was also used to heat the rooms through an underfloor system.

The palace is open daily, 10 am - 6 pm.

— Palace of the Shirvanshahs back to the Double Gates —

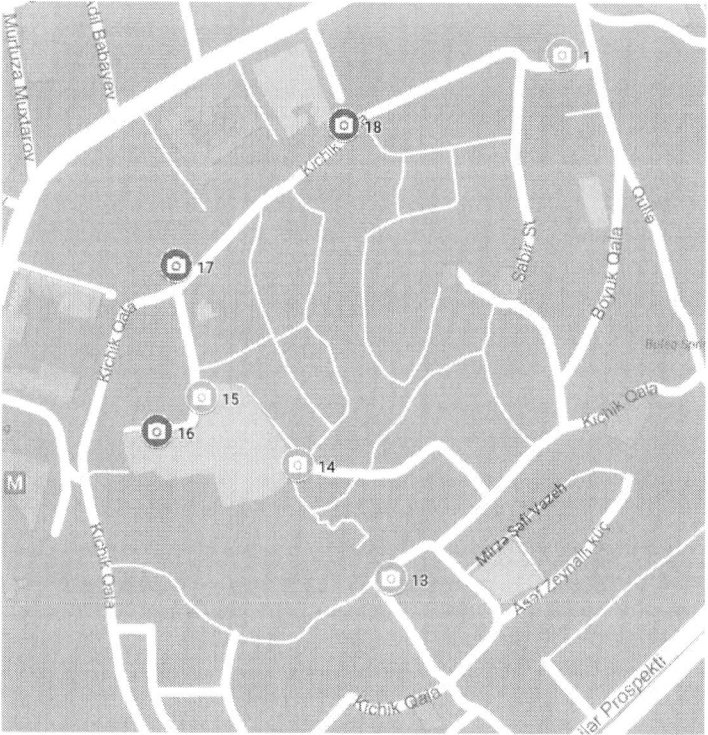

Map D | Palace of the Shirvanshahs back to the Double Gates

Once you have finished your visit to the Palace of the Shirvanshahs, turn left from the main entrance. Follow the road down the slight incline and around the bend. On the right-hand side is the Museum of Miniature Books *(Map D, Point 16)*.

Museum of Miniature Books

This unique museum, supposedly the only one of its kind in the world, opened its doors in 2002. Its founder, Zarifa Salahova, is the daughter of the decorated Azerbaijani artist Tahir Salahov, and over the years she has built a collection of 6,500 books.

On display are many tiny volumes from distinguished Azerbaijaini and Soviet authors, as well as the works of the giants of Western literature such as Shakespeare, Hemingway and Conan Doyle. The oldest piece on display is a seventeenth-century Qur'an.

A highlight of the collection, and the most extreme example of miniaturisation are three of the world's tiniest books, each measuring just 2 mm by 2 mm. To read them a powerful magnifying glass is required.

The museum is open Tuesdays to Sundays from 10 am to 5 pm, and entrance is free.

Old walls

From the museum, retrace your steps back past the Palace of the Shirvanshahs and head straight, until you reach the old city walls *(Map D, Point 17)*, then turn right. You can then follow these walls all the way back to the Double Gates. On the way, there are opportunities to walk along a path at the top of the walls, and there are various canons and siege-weapons to admire, such as a fearsome giant catapult.

* * *

Quadrangular tower

A short walk along the twelfth-century walls you will encounter a much taller and heavily fortified quadrangular tower *(Map D, Point 18)*, also known as the Donjon. 18 m high and with 2 m thick walls, this tower was used throughout the Middle Ages as an armoury and as a powerful defensive feature. Inside, a spiral staircase links four floors.

There is some debate regarding the tower's age. Some believe that it was built at the same time as the adjoining walls. However, others point to accounts written by the court poet, Badr Shirvani, who specifically noted its construction in 1428-29.

Archaeological excavations in the tower have unearthed quite complex architectural features such as an integral well and a sanitation and ventilation system.

Back to the Double Gates

From the quadrangular tower, continue to follow the street, Kichik Qala, until the T-junction. At this point, turn left, and you will find yourself back at the Double Gates, where this walking tour ends.

Baku Walking Tour 2 - Boom Town

In the nineteenth century, Baku was at the very heart of the global oil trade. Forget Saudi Arabia and the Gulf states, Azerbaijan produced well over half of the world's entire oil. As you'd expect, this resulted in rivers of hard currency flowing rapidly into the region. Baku boomed accordingly, and between 1850 and the turn of the century its population exploded, growing faster than London or New York.

Many people grew incredibly rich overnight, and a new oil baron class wanted to show off their wealth. They built hundreds of luxurious mansions, designed by some of the best architects and using architectural styles from all over the world. New avenues were laid out to accommodate this upsurge in construction, and oil baron money supported the creation of new public parks and gardens, concert halls, libraries and theatres.

As the old city was already full, this development rippled outwards from the ancient walls. It created a new cityscape that would have been worthy of London, Paris or any other global city. However, the boom time was destined not to last forever, and in 1920 the Bolsheviks took power in Baku. All this opulent private property was seized and converted into many different apartments for the masses. The oil barons fled as fast as they could.

The good news is that much of this boom time architecture survived the Soviet period, and this walking tour looks at some of the best survivors of that time.

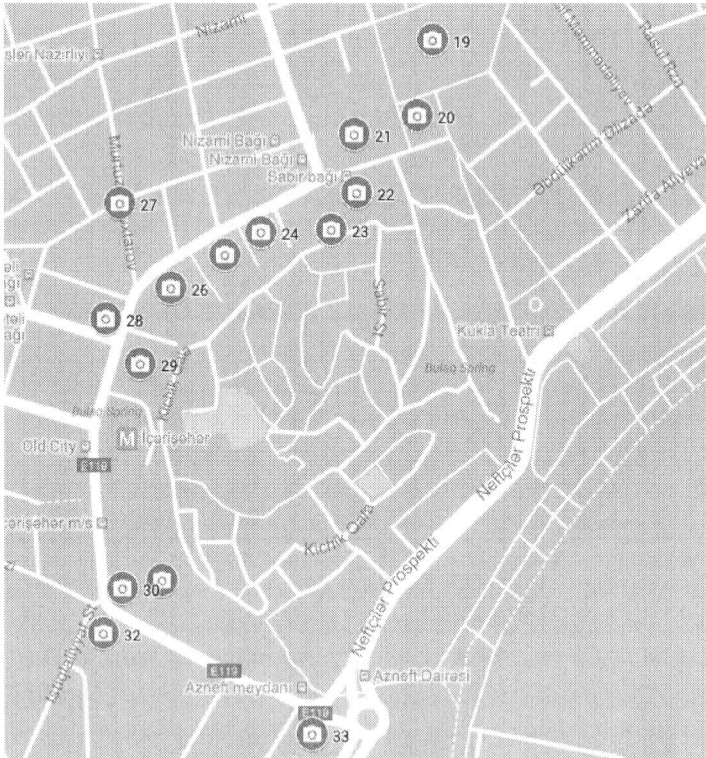

Map E | Boom Town

Fountain Square

This walking tour begins in the leafy surroundings of Fountain Square *(Map E, Point 19)*, built in the mid-nineteenth century. In Soviet times this expansive public space was named after the revolutionary socialist Karl Marx, however, following the construction of many fountains during the 1980s, and independence in 1991, it became popularly known as Fountain Square.

Today this area is a favourite meeting place, particularly after work and at the weekends, and draws its fair share of tourists too. Shops, restaurants and cafes surround the square. Keep your eyes open for two charming modern statues depicting typical Baku residents. The one outside McDonald's shows a young woman on a mobile phone sheltering under an umbrella, and another next to a fountain shows another young lady this time busy putting on her lipstick. You won't be able to miss them as there is a steady stream of people taking selfies with them.

Nizami Museum of Literature

Exit the square in the southwestern corner where you see a two-storey KFC, and you will find the grand Nizami Museum of Literature *(Map E, Point 20)* on your left. This institution preserves and showcases the literature of Azerbaijan. Even before entering this museum, you get a sense of the pride in the country's literary heroes. The magnificent facade of this museum features six imposing statues of the most accomplished Azerbaijani writers and poets, housed in monumental alcoves. The statues show Fizuli, Vagif, Akhundov, Natavan, Mammadguluzade and Jabbarli. The museum takes its name from the most honoured national poet, Nizami Ganjavi. Born in Azerbaijan during the twelfth century, Nizami is considered to be the greatest poet in Persian literature. In addition to having national treasure status in his home country, poetry lovers across Iran, Afghanistan, Kurdistan and Tajikistan revere him.

The building has had a chequered history. It was initially built as a one-storey caravanserai in 1850. Later, at the height of the oil boom, one of the new millionaires, Haji Hajagha Dadashov, purchased the caravanserai, adding a second floor and banqueting room to create the much grander and luxurious Metropol Hotel. Its life in the hospitality was shortlived, however, thanks to the Bolsheviks and for the next couple of decades was occupied by the Trade Union Committee of Azerbaijan. In 1939, on the 800th birthday of Nizami, the government decided to convert the building into a Museum of Literature. Work began, and in 1943 the facade was redesigned to include the six statues you see today. In 1945 the museum's doors opened.

Nizami Park and Monument

Directly across the street from the main facade of the Nizam Museum of Literature, is the Nizami Park *(Map E, Point 21)*. A grand staircase, flanked by willow trees, leads up the slight hill, to a statue of Nizami himself. It was installed at this spot in 1949, created by the People's Artist of Azerbaijan, Fuad Abdurahmanov, a renowned sculptor responsible for many monumental statues around Baku. If you look back towards the Museum of Literature, the statue of Fizuli was also a work by Abdurahmanov.

This statue of Nizami is 6 m high and made from bronze. It stands on an octagonal red granite pedestal, each side of which has bronze plates showing scenes from some of Nizami's most famous works.

Sabir Park and Monument

When facing the Nizami monument, turn to your left, cross the street, and you'll be in Sabir Park *(Map E, Point 22)*. The focal point of this green space nestling under the old city walls is a statue of the Azerbaijani satirical poet and philosopher, Mirza Alakbar Sabir (1862-1911).

In the first decade of the twentieth century, Sabir was at his most productive, writing extensively for satirical publications. He was mainly involved with the Molla Nasraddin magazine, whose publisher was Jalil Mammadguluzade, also one of the six statues on the facade of the Museum of Literature.

Sabir's work was popular with the working classes throughout the country, as his writing exposed the foibles of Tsarist administrators, greedy landowners, backward clergy and the plight of downtrodden women. His poverty resulted in his early death in 1911.

Taghiyev Gate and Old City Walls

The old city walls form an imposing backdrop to Sabir Park. Slightly to the east of the Sabir statue is the beautiful arched Taghiyev Gate *(Map E, Point 23)*, giving direct access to the Old Town. However, not is all as it seems, and this gate is not a twelfth-century portal but one that was built somewhat more recently in 1877 by Haji Zeynalabdin Taghiyev.

Taghiyev was a local merchant who owned some shops which stood where Sabir Park is today. However, he had great difficulty renting these shops out, because they were thought to be too far from the main bazaar in the old city. So Taghiyev asked permission from Baku city council to break through the old city walls at that point, and erect a new gate to create a shortcut. In those days before the advent of cultural conservation and UNESCO, the council agreed, and the portal was built. Taghiyev's businesses duly flourished.

In 1918, there was a battle at this site when the Armenians were trying to capture the Baku. Taghiyev's son led the inner city defenders and successfully managed to repel the invaders.

Ismailiyya Palace

From Sabir Park, walk west along Istiglaliyyat Street. This thoroughfare is one of the oldest and most prestigious in the entire city, with its name meaning 'independence' or 'sovereignty'. Today it is lined with palaces, universities, government offices and upscale shops and restaurants.

The very first building on the left side is one of the grandest and most ornate of the oil baron mansions, the Ismailiyya Palace *(Map E, Point 24)*, built by the wealthy oil magnate, Musa Naghiyev. While he was widely believed to be the most tight-fisted millionnaire in the city, he went on to create this most lavish palace in the Venetian Gothic style. It was designed to commemorate his deceased son, Ismail, and Naghiyev donated it to the Muslim Charity Society in 1913.

During the 1918 conflict with Armenia, the palace suffered significant fire damage and required extensive restoration in the early part of the 1920s. As part of this reconstruction, the original Islamic motifs which featured on the facade were replaced by the then more ideologically correct Soviet stars. Today, the building houses the Presidium of the Academy of Sciences.

Capitals of the Caucasus

* * *

The Institute of Manuscripts

Millionnaire philanthropist Haji Zeynalabdin Taghiyev constructed this grand building *(Map E, Point 25)* at the turn of the twentieth century. Do not confuse this man with the merchant who built the gate in the old city walls by Sabir Park. Over time, there have been five separate individuals of note in Baku with the same name!

This Taghiyev was born into an impoverished family in Baku, and from an early age worked as a bricklayer. He slowly saved up his money, and during the oil boom invested in the oil business. He used his vast profits to build a diversified business empire spanning shipbuilding, energy, forestry, fishing, banking and real estate. In addition to being an astute businessman, he was involved in many civic projects and funded city trams, theatres and water pipelines.

Taghiyev became increasingly concerned about the closed lives of Muslim girls and their lack of education. He sent his daughters to St Petersburg for schooling, but he wanted people with less means to educate their daughters in Baku. This inspired him to construct a dedicated school for Muslim girls at his own expense. The building, which now houses the Institute of Manuscripts, was completed in 1901 and named the Alexandra School for Girls after the Russian Empress and wife of Nicholas II.

In 1920, the invading Bolsheviks commandeered the building into a headquarters for 'worker, peasant and soldier deputies', and after that housed the Supreme Soviet of the Azerbaijan Republic.

Today's institute collects and catalogues old books and manuscripts which hold particular interest to the nation of Azerbaijan, to the broader region and for Islam. Some of its most treasured artefacts are Azerbaijani medical and pharmaceutical-related manuscripts from the twelfth century. The gem of the entire collection is a complete manuscript of "Khamsa", a poetry collection penned by Nizami, a seventeenth-century copy of the twelfth-century original.

Azerbaijan State University of Economics

The next big edifice along the left side of Istiglaliyyat Street is the Azerbaijan State University of Economics *(Map E, Point 26)*. Founded in 1930, this is one of the largest educational institutions in the whole of the Caucasus with 18,000 students and one thousand teachers split across nine faculties.

The classic Azerbaijani novel, Ali and Nino by Kurban Said, opens in a classroom in this very building.

Wedding Palace

To see another stunning example of an early twentieth-century oil baron's mansion, try to cross the busy Istiglaliyyat Street (there is an underpass further along if this proves too difficult), and make a quick detour up Murtuza Mukhtarov Street to the junction with Ahmed Cavad Street.

Here on the corner, you will see a magnificent French gothic mansion *(Map E, Point 27)* built in 1911 by the oil baron Murtuza Mukhtarov, after whom the street was eventually named. He made the lavish house as a surprise present for his wife, replicating a manor she fell in love with while travelling in France.

A sweet love story, yet one that eventually ended in tragedy. In 1920, when the Bolsheviks invaded Baku,

Mukhtarov forbade them to go inside his wife's precious house with their heavy military boots. However, not only did they enter but they did so on horseback. The humiliated oil baron shot three of them before shooting himself. His wife managed to escape to Istanbul.

During Soviet times, as it is today, the building is used for marriage registrations, so the love story still lives on!

Nariman Narimanov Museum

Retrace your steps back down Murtuza Mukhtarov Street to its junction with Istiglaliyyat Street and turn right. After a short block, you will come to the museum dedicated to the life and times of Nariman Narimanov *(Map E, Point 28)*, the Azerbaijani Bolshevik, writer, doctor and statesman.

Born in 1870, Narimanov's early plays and stories focused on highlighting outdated customs, traditions and religious practices, and called for their abandonment. He also stood up for the rights of hard done by local peasants. When the 1905 revolution burst into life, Narimanov immediately joined the Bolshevik party, leading various movements and protests. As a result, the authorities exiled him to Astrakhan for five years. After the 1917 revolution, Narimanov became the leader of the Azerbaijani social democratic party, which was to become the Azerbaijan communist party, and in 1920-21 headed the government of Soviet Azerbaijan.

His importance is undelrined by Leon Tolstoy, who called his death the most significant loss to the eastern world after Lenin. His ashes were given the honour of being interred in the Kremlin walls in Moscow. Today you can see many streets, parks and buildings named after him all over Azerbaijan, and even across Russia.

The museum consists of the four rooms of the apartment in

which Narimanov lived from 1913-18. The exhibits comprise documents and materials relating to his early life, political career, writing and family.

City Hall

Crossing back to the other side of Istiglaliyyat Street, the impressive Baroque building to the right of the university is the Baku City Hall *(Map E, Point 29)*. Three stories with a grand clock tower and red decorative bricks and marble imported from Italy, the City hall contains the residence of the mayor, various other public staterooms and the session hall.

Philharmonic Hall and Fountain Park

Continuing down Istiglaliyyat Street, you will pass the red line Metro station Icherisheher. A few metres further on, on the left-hand side where the street curves around, is the Azerbaijan State Philharmonic Hall *(Map E, Point 30)*.

It was built in 1910-12 in an ornate Italian Renaissance style inspired by the l'Opera de Monte Carlo and is yet another clear example of the effect copious oil dollars had during the boom years. After a renovation in 1993, the building took its name from the famous Azerbaijani composer and conductor, Muslim Magomayev.

The interior is predominantly German Rococo and comprises a Summer Hall with one thousand seats and a Winter Hall seating 610. It is now home to state orchestras, choirs, dance troupes and folk music organisations.

Just behind the Philharmonic Hall is one of Baku's oldest and most beautiful green spaces, the Fountain Park *(Map E,*

Point 31). This has a French baroque fountain, surrounded by an elegant, whitewashed arched colonnade, and is a popular rendezvous point for young couples. Even Ali and Nino met here! There are fantastic views to be had; the old city walls form a dramatic backdrop, the Flame Towers poke their heads above the trees at various points, and the whole park slopes gently down to the sparkling waters of the Caspian Sea. It's a relaxing and peaceful place to pause on any tour around Baku.

National Art Museum of Azerbaijan

Just across Niyazi Street from the Philharmonic Hall is the National Art Museum of Azerbaijan *(Map E, Point 32)*. The museum spreads across two buildings standing next to each other.

The first building, which is on your left side as you view the museum from the street, was originally built as an oil boom mansion for De Bour of Rothschilds, the company that eventually became Shell. Another famous resident of this mansion was the prominent Bolshevik Nariman Narimanov. The second building, just up the hill next to the President's office, was originally a secondary school for Russian girls.

There are sixty rooms in the whole museum, thirty in each building, displaying more than 3000 items. The European collection includes works by a diverse selection of sixteenth to nineteenth century Italian, Flemish, German and Russian painters. The Azerbaijani section features art from the last century from prominent local painters, as well as ancient ceramics and metalwork.

In a small back courtyard there are bullet-ridden statues of the Azerbaijani composer Uzeyir Hajibeyov, singer Bulbul and poet Natavan. These were displayed in the town of

Shusha in Nagorno-Karabakh, considered the cultural heartland of Azerbaijan, and were used as target practice by Armenian troops.

The museum is open Tuesdays to Sundays, and the entrance fee is 10 Manat for foreigners and 5 Manat for locals.

SOCAR

From the museum, stroll down Niyazi Street towards the Caspian. At the end of the street, fronting the Neftchilar Prospect, is the vast three-storey oil boom mansion home to SOCAR *(Map E, Point 33)*, the State Oil Company of the Azerbaijan Republic.

The building was built in 1896 and was purchased in the early 1900s by Mir Babayev, a local folk singer, which brings us to another story of how oil can change someone's fortunes overnight. Mir Babeyev was a folk singer with a magnificent voice, who began to be invited to perform at oil baron weddings. At one such event, he so deeply moved the immensely wealthy relatives of the groom that he was given oil-producing land as a lavish gift. Very soon he was producing thousands of barrels of oil and expanded his operation to include three more oil fields and eighteen oil rigs. With his new found wealth he purchased the building which now houses SOCAR. He lived there in splendour until 1920, when he fled the country following the Bolshevik take over.

Today, SOCAR has outgrown the venerable old building and has constructed a massive new skyscraper further out on Heydar Aliyev Avenue. It is the tallest in Azerbaijan and is set to become a brand new landmark for the city, rivalling the Flame Towers.

This is the endpoint of this walking tour.

Baku Walking Tour 3 - Parks and Panoramas

Funicular

From the endpoint of the previous walking tour, the SOCAR building, walk south along Neftchilar Prospect, with the Caspian Sea on your left, for about 200 m, and then turn right up Shovkat Alakbarova. The Funicular station *(Map F, Point 34)* will be directly ahead, and the starting point of the next walking tour, Parks and Panoramas.

* * *

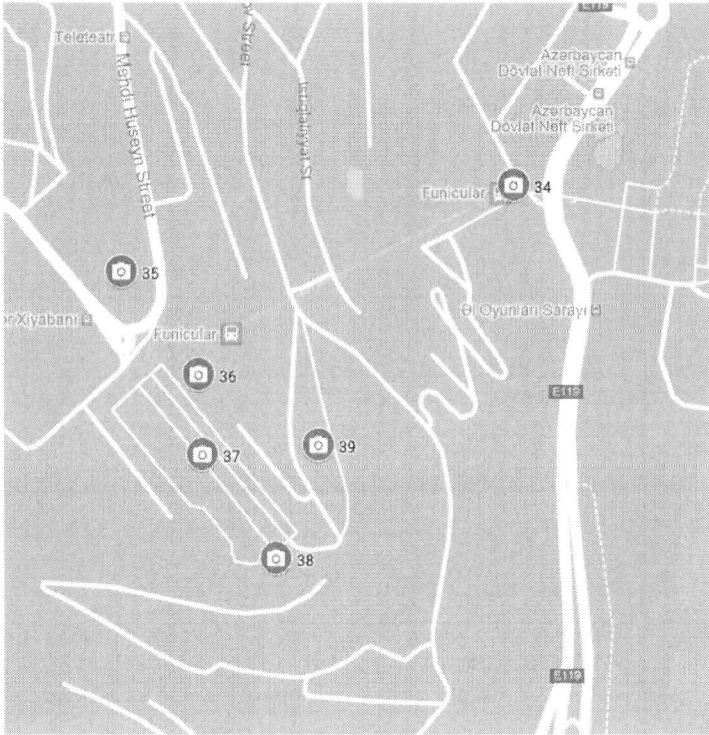

Map F: Parks and Panoramas

The Funicular connects Neftchilar Prospect with Dagestu Park and saves a long, steep climb up the hill. The railway track is just under half a kilometre long, and the train leaves approximately every ten minutes throughout the day between 10 am and 10 pm.

The lower station is named Bahram Gur, after the mythical Azerbaijani hero. You can see his statue directly in front of the station in a fountain pool, which depicts the hero using a giant sword to slay a fierce dragon. This character comes from Nizami's poem, "Seven Beauties". The upper station is named Shehidler Xiyabani, the Azerbaijani translation of

"Martyr's Lane" found in Upland Park.

On the journey up the hill, you can get panoramic views of Baku and the Caspian Sea through the train's large windows.

Flame Towers

This trio of skyscrapers *(Map F, Point 35)* is the most prominent landmark of Baku and can be glimpsed from all over the city, forming a futuristic backdrop. When you walk out of the upper Funicular station, you get to see the towers up close.

The buildings, reaching up to a height of 182 m, house apartments, offices, and the luxurious five-star Fairmont Hotel. The long history of fire worship in Baku inspires their design, and from any vantage point, the distinctive curved shapes of the towers appear as three massive flames. They rest on a triangular podium which comprises leisure facilities, restaurants, cafes, cinemas, shops and parking.

More than ten thousand LED lights cover the towers, and at night they turn into massive LED display screens and can be seen from the furthest points of the city.

Between the Funicular station and the Flame Towers is the Shehidlar Khiyabani mosque, and this juxtaposition of the more traditional face of Baku with twenty-first-century architecture makes for some memorable photos.

Upland Park

This green space *(Map F, Point 36)* is pretty much the highest point of Baku and is a beautiful and serene place to take a stroll. From the Funicular station, wander through the park with the Flame Towers on your right-hand side. There are many scenic spots to take photos. In particular, look out for the spectacular man-made waterfall feature.

Shehidlar Xiyabani (Martyr's Lane)

Located directly behind the waterfall, Martyr's Lane *(Map F, Point 37)* is a cemetery and memorial dedicated to those who died in two recent violent events, Black January and the Nagorno Karabakh War.

The cemetery has had a somewhat chequered past. It was established in 1918 as a Muslim cemetery, and initially contained the bodies of those killed in localised fighting of the Russian Civil War. However, when the Bolsheviks came to power in 1920, the cemetery was destroyed, the bodies removed and replaced by an amusement park. It was only after the collapse of the Soviet Union that the government reinstated the graveyard for the victims of recent conflicts.

Today, you can find the graves of 15,000 people here. White marble walls line the main central avenue, in front of which are black marble tombstones, each with a photo of the fallen. All have the same date of death - 20 January 1990 - the day of the Black January massacre. On this winter's weekend, the Soviet Red Army invaded Baku to quash a growing independence movement. Much cruelty accompanied the invasion, and historians estimate that the invaders killed three hundred. The atrocity only served to strength Azerbaijan's resolve, and the country achieved independence the following year.

Slightly further up the hill, in the shade of trees, are the graves of those killed in the Nagorno Karabakh War. This conflict lasted from 1988 to 1994 and saw ethnic Armenians of the Nagorno Karabakh region, backed by Armenia, fighting for independence from Azerbaijan. Over the years of persistent struggle, 30,000 people lost their lives. 1992 seems to have been a particularly bad year, as it repeatedly appears on the gravestones.

Shehidlar Monument

At the southeastern point end of the Martyrs Lane is the Shehidlar Monument *(Map F, Point 38)*, built in 1998 by the order of then-president Heydar Aliyev. This elegant open-sided tower stands over an eternal flame, issuing from a golden eight-pointed star. Another identical golden star on the apex of the monument's dome represents the spirits of those martyrs who sacrificed their lives for their country.

Dagustu Park

As you walk away from the monument, with the Caspian Sea on your right, you are now in Dagustu Park *(Map F, Point 39)*. The walkway along the ridge affords spectacular panoramic views of the city and sea. In the distance on the extreme left is the angular profile of the Baku Crystal Hall, built to host the Eurovision Song Contest, and the adjacent huge national flagpole. Looking further to the left you can take in the entire corniche, old city, business district and a big slice of the Absheron peninsula.

Once back down at the Bahram Gur Funicular station, you can begin the next perambulation, Corniche and Commerce.

Baku Walking Tour 4 - Corniche and Commerce

Next to the statue of Bahram Gur is a subway leading under the busy Neftchilar Prospect. Once on the other side of the road, you are confronted with the distinctive shape of the Carpet Museum.

* * *

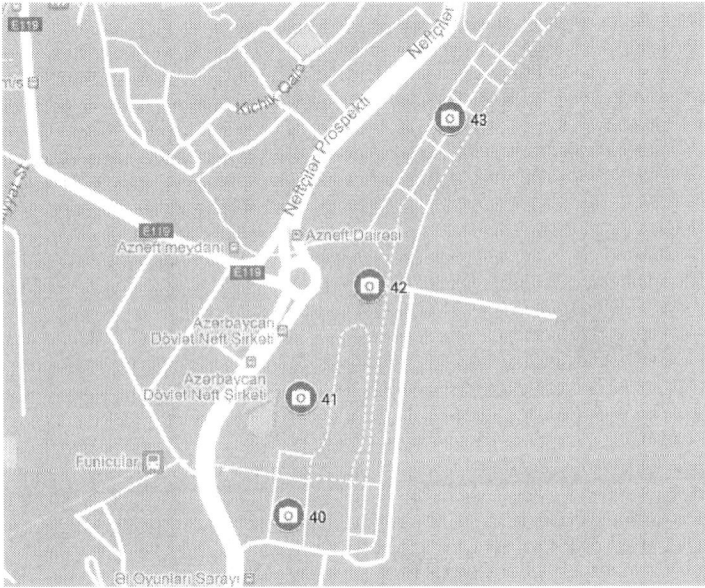

Map G | Carpet Museum and along Baku Boulevard

Carpet Museum

The Azerbaijan Carpet Museum *(Map G, Point 40)* was established in 1967 but has only just moved into its distinctive building, which takes the form of a gigantic carpet being rolled out, in 2014.

The museum is purportedly the only one in the world dedicated to the art of carpet weaving. It has the most extensive collection of Azerbaijani carpets anywhere, and safeguards for the nation more than 10,000 objects. Azerbaijani carpets are held dear to the heart of national culture, and UNESCO has recently declared that they are a "Masterpiece of Intangible Heritage". The museum plays a crucial role in their preservation and research and aims to further the knowledge of residents and visitors of this cultural treasure.

The museum takes its name from Latif Karimov, a scientist, artist and carpet weaver who showed how the carpet has the most profound connection to the history and culture of Azerbaijan. He made an immense contribution to the research and classification of carpets and led a revival in their making. The culmination of Karimov's work was the establishment of the museum in 1967. Twenty-six years later it was named after him.

Most of the carpets on display date from the seventeenth century onwards, and include flat-woven and pile carpets. A lot of information is presented as to how the carpets are made and how techniques and patterns differ between various regions. It is surprisingly fascinating, and while the notion of a carpet museum might bring up images of dusty, dull exhibitions, the opposite is the case. You can spend an informative couple of hours here.

In the basement of the museum is a small vault containing exquisite examples of Azerbaijan jewellery and metalwork, mostly from the last two hundred years but some from as far back as the bronze age.

The museum is open Tuesdays to Fridays from 10 am to 6 pm, with extended hours on Saturdays and Sundays from 10 am to 8 pm. The entrance fee is 7 Manat.

Little Venice

Directly in front of the Carpet Museum on the Corniche is Little Venice *(Map G, Point 41)*. Dating from the 1960s, this mini version of the glorious Italian city is replete with canals, elegant bridges, Venetian colonnades and, of course, gondolas. The town has two large islands and several small islets, each with a selection of restaurants, bars and cafes. It's a lovely venue for lunch and dinner, or merely to rest one's weary feet.

Bayraq

Walk 100 m north along the corniche. Here is the Bayraq *(Map G, Point 42)*, or national flagpole, not to be confused with another Bayraq at the southern end of the corniche, which once held the Guinness World Record as being the world's tallest flagpole. This bayraq faces the SOCAR building across the Neftchilar Prospect. Here, you can take Instagram-worthy photos of the national flag fluttering away with the Flame Towers in the background.

Azerbaijan's national flag is a blue-red-green tricolour with crescent moon and star in the middle and was adopted in 1918. However, the Bolshevik takeover in 1920 and subsequent integration into the Soviet Union meant that the flag didn't fly again until independence in 1991. The blue colour represents the Turkic origin and heritage of Azerbaijanis, the red symbolises modernisation and development, while the green expresses adherence to the Islamic religion. The crescent in the centre again links to Turkism, and the eight-pointed star refers to the eight guiding principles of the founder of the Azerbaijan Republic, Mammad Amin Rasulzade.

Baku Boulevard

From the flagpole, the wide Baku Boulevard and park *(Map G, Point 43)* runs parallel to Neftchilar Prospect and the shore of the Caspian Sea. This promenade traces its history back to the oil boom times in the late nineteenth century. At that time, Neftchilar Prospect was built to connect the oil fields in Bibi Heybat with the city. The oil barons built their mansions along one side, and the Caspian Sea was on the other. Over the years, the land on the seaward side was reclaimed inch by inch, with tons of fertile soil being imported to create the parkland seen today. The entire stretch now has National Park protected status and is a favourite place to stroll, jog, enjoy the fresh air and enjoy views of the sea and cityscape. Dotted along its length are pleasant cafes.

Map H | Baku Boulevard to Fountain Square

Halfway along the boulevard is the Parachute Tower *(Map H, Point 44)*, a 75 m high structure built in 1936 to resemble an oil derrick. Such towers were common at that time throughout the USSR, and as the name suggests were used for parachute jumping. Anyone could use it, not just the military, and you could opt to jump from ten, twenty, twenty-five or sixty-metre platforms, depending on your appetite for risk. Unfortunately, one of the jumpers died in an accident, and parachuting stopped soon after that. Nowadays, the tower is used to display the time, date, temperature and wind speed to those passing by underneath.

A five to ten-minute walk up the boulevard is the Park Bulvar shopping mall *(Map H, Point 45)*, offering high-end stores with many top brands.

Freedom Square and Government House

Just past the Park Bulvar mall is the Freedom Square *(Map H, Point 46)*, the biggest such public space in Baku. Built in the 1960s, the square was originally called Lenin Square and was home to a Lenin statue, removed after independence in 1991. The space now plays a vital role in the public life of Azerbaijan and hosts the annual independence day celebrations and military parades.

Fronting onto this square is the sprawling Stalinist bulk of Government House *(Map H, Point 47)*, built between 1936 and 1952 to house more than five thousand public servants. Today it is home to a variety of ministries, including those looking after tourism, agriculture, labour and procurement portfolios.

On either side of Government House are top-end hotels such as the Hilton and JW Marriott.

Retail therapy on Nizami Street

From Baku Boulevard, cross to the other side of Neftchilar Prospect using the pedestrian underpass found to the side of the Park Bulvar mall. Walk straight up Zadliq Prospect, past the Hilton Hotel, until you reach the junction with Nizami Street, at which point you should turn left.

Nizami Street *(Map H, Point 48)*, named after the famous Azerbaijani poet, is the most famous and glamorous shopping street of Baku, akin to London's Oxford Street or Paris' Champs Elysees. The real estate here is among some of the most expensive in the world. The main shopping area stretches from here all the way to Fountain Square, and as it is pedestrianised along its full length, it makes for a relaxing place to stroll and do some window shopping.

As well as the myriad retail opportunities, the other draw of Nizami Street is the architecture. Buildings here feature a variety of architecture including baroque, renaissance, neogothic and post-modern. There is something to please every taste.

Once you reach the ISR Plaza building, turn left, and after a few metres you will be in Fountain Square, where this walking tour concludes.

Day Trips from Baku

— Ateshgah Fire Temple —

The Ateshgah Fire Temple, further out on the Absheron peninsula, makes for a fascinating afternoon getaway from the city. It is an ancient site of Zoroastrian worship, and its name in Persian means 'Home of Fire'.

For centuries Zoroastrianism was the dominant religion of Azerbaijan, and evidence shows that it was extensively practised even as far back as the first millennium BC. The belief was also widespread in Iran before its eventual conversion to Islam. Once Azerbaijan became part of the Persian empire, various emperors such as Cyrus II and Darius I played an essential role in spreading Zoroastrianism across their empire. Even today, well-preserved temples can be seen in the Iranian cities of Yazd and Esfahan.

Zoroastrianism has the distinction of being the world's first monotheistic religion and takes its name from its founder, the Persian prophet Zoroaster. Adherents to the faith worshipped a god called Ahura Mazda, and fire was the most important symbol of the religion as it was considered to represent his holy spirit.

The Ateshgah fire temple complex is pentagonal. The five sides comprise a series of cells, chapels and a caravanserai, and these now house an exhibition that ponders the origin and purpose of the temple. In the middle of the central courtyard is the main fire temple altar, built directly over a natural gas vent.

The current form of this fire temple dates from the seventeenth century, although there is evidence that religious activity at this site stretched back much further in time. So why does this particular site hold so much importance to Zoroastrians? The answer is in the ground. This part of Azerbaijan has massive subterranean natural gas reserves, and in some place these bubble up to the surface and spontaneously combust into flame. For an ancient Zoroastrian, this would have seemed like a holy site, and followers would of course want to worship in such a place. Even today, just up the road at Yanar Dag, a hillside continues to burn due to this natural outpouring of gas.

After the introduction of Islam into the area, the ancient temples standing on this site were either destroyed or fell into ruin. However, activity at the site began to reoccur from the fifteenth century onwards, due to the strengthening of overland trade routes between the Caspian and the Subcontinent. Indian travellers and merchants soon made pilgrimages to the site, and at the turn of the eighteenth century began construction of religious buildings, some of which remain today. There is some dispute as to whether Zoroastrians or Hindus used the temple - fire is important to both religions - and displays inside the various cells and rooms of the temple complex present all sides of the argument. It is fascinating nonetheless to see a unique mix of

Sanskrit, Punjabi and Persian inscriptions throughout the temple.

In the mid-nineteenth-century, the gas supply became irregular due to geological movements, and the flame was no longer so constant. Worshippers took this as a sign of their god's displeasure, and they eventually abandoned the site in 1880. In the 1960s the gas ran out altogether, and the bright flames you see burning today are less romantically piped in by Baku's main gas supply.

Getting to Ateshgah Fire Temple

The temple *(Map I, Point 49)* is in the town of Surakhani, one of Baku's more farther-flung suburbs. The quickest way to get there is by hiring a taxi to take you directly there. You will need to negotiate with the driver to wait for you and then drop you back, as taxis are not easily found there, or will ask for high fares.

* * *

Map I | Ateshgah Fire Temple

However, a much more fun, and significantly cheaper option is to take public transport all the way there. It gives you a real insight into how ordinary Azerbaijanis go about their business each day and is a highlight of a visit to Baku. Here is a summary of how to do it:

- Catch a red line metro. In the centre of Baku, the most convenient stations are the Icherisheher (old town) next to the Philharmonic Park, and Sahil a couple of hundred metres east of Fountain Square. Make sure that the train is going in the direction of Hazi Aslanov.
- To get on the metro, you first need to by a 'Bakucard'

in the ticket hall. You can buy a card for extended use, which you can top up with cash, or one for limited use (1-4 rides). The cost of a ride is 0.20 AZN.

- Get off the train at Koroglu metro station. There are a few exits to this station, and you should make sure that you exit on the south side of the highway with traffic going away from the city (the Olympic Stadium is to the north)

- The Koroglu bus station is just the side of the highway with dozens of buses randomly parked all over the place. Look out for bus number 184 and hop on. The fare is 0.2 AZN. Don't worry about missing your stop. Just stay on until the bus route's terminus at Surakhani railway station.

- Cross the railway lines behind the station, looking out for the odd stray train as you do so!

- The Ateshgah Fire Temple is on your left at the end of the road.

Back to Baku

When returning to Baku, get another bus 184 from the same bus stop at the railway station. On the way back to the city the bus passes through a genuinely dystopian paradise of industrial-scale decay. Hundreds, if not thousands of rusting, poorly maintained 'nodding donkey' oil pumps line the road, interspersed with ageing electricity pylons and piles of discarded, oily machinery. If you are an environmentalist, it is best to look away. For movie buffs, this is where scenes of 'The World is Not Enough' was filmed, with Pierce Brosnan starring as secret agent James Bond. There are reports that local police are not keen on tourists taking photos were, so it is best to be discreet.

Once the bus stops at Koroglu metro station, get the red line back to the centre of town.

— Yanar Dag —

Yanar Dag *(Map J, Point 50)* is a dramatic natural gas flare which burns continuously on a hillside north of Baku between the villages of Digah and Mammedli. In Azerbaijani, the name Yanar Dag means burning mountainside. Flames shoot up between about 1 m and 2 m in the air and are particularly impressive at sunset or nighttime. The fire results from natural gas seeping out of the ground and then spontaneously combusting. There is a strong smell of gas in the air, and locals say that nearby streams can be ignited with a match. Maybe best not to smoke around here!

Such flames were once widespread throughout the Absheron peninsula, and Marco Polo even wrote about seeing them in the thirteenth century. These fires are the same phenomenon that once occurred at the site of the Ateshgah Fire Temple, and resulted in the spread of Zoroastrianism in the region. Today, due to the exploitation of oil and gas, reserves are much depleted, and Yanar Dag is now very much an oddity.

* * *

Capitals of the Caucasus

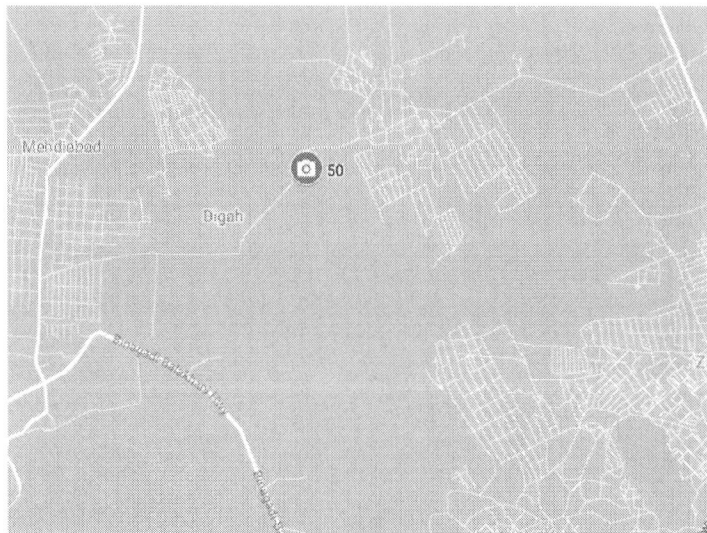

Map J: Yanar Dag

To get to Yanar Dag, you can catch a red line metro to Koroglu. Then take bus 217 from Koroglu metro station. Stay on the bus to its terminus. As both the Ateshgah Fire Temple and Yanar Dag are reached by different buses from this metro station, you could combine both destinations in one day trip.

— Heydar Aliyev Centre —

The Heydar Aliyev Centre *(Map K, Point 51)* is a mammoth cultural centre a bit out of the city centre towards the northeast. The building itself is a star attraction, and worth visiting even if you do not venture inside. The structure is designed by the lauded late architect, Zaha Hadid, and is regarded as one of her true masterpieces, even standing out from the many other fantastic buildings she created around the world.

The building has no sharp angles at all and instead comprises swooping sinuous curves which some have compared to a mountain range of whipped cream. Others have likened it to Marilyn Monroe's blown skirt. Whatever you think it resembles or stands for, it is one of those buildings that will inspire you and stay with you for a long time.

Inside, the design ethos continues, with light, airy spaces and flowing lines. The centre houses an auditorium, gallery, hall and museum, and aims to act as the beating heart of Baku's cultural and intellectual life.

The three-floor museum describes Azerbaijani history and the life and work of former President Heydar Aliyev, from whom the centre takes its name. The museum hosts many temporary exhibitions throughout the year.

* * *

Capitals of the Caucasus

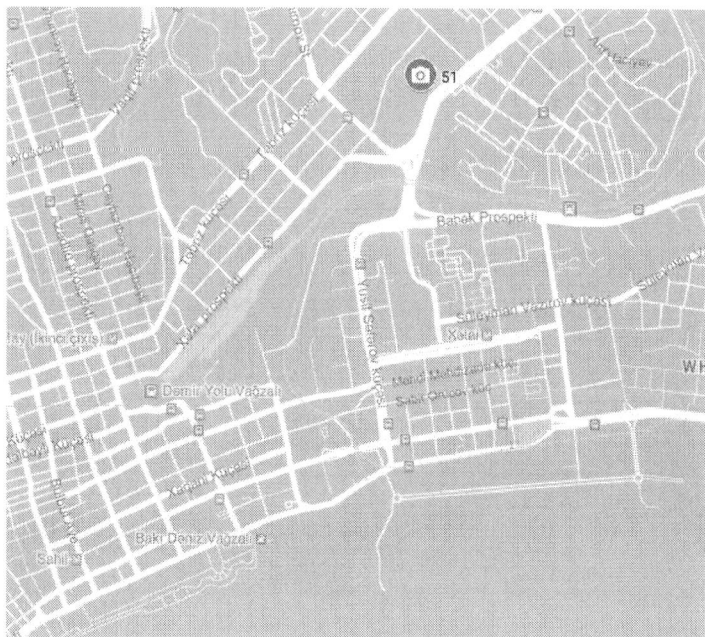

Map K: Heydar Aliyev Centre

The Heyday Aliyev Centre is open from Tuesday to Sundays, from 11 am to 6 pm. A standard ticket, available online, costs 15 Manat. To get there from the centre of Baku, there are frequent services on a variety of bus lines, including buses 1 and 2. Visit www.bakubus.az for the latest routes and timetables; the site is available in English.

— Gobustan National Park —

Located 60 km southwest of Baku, this national park is famed for two things you are unlikely to find elsewhere on your travels: petroglyphs and mud volcanoes. The park is an easy day trip from the city, and you can use one of the many travel agencies offering tours there, or hire a taxi.

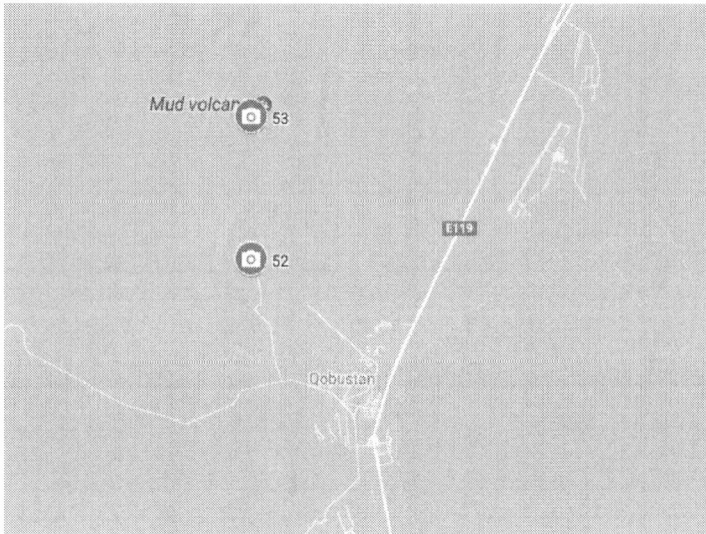

Map L | Gobustan National Park

Petroglyphs (Map L, Point 52)

Petroglyphs are drawings, etched into rock outcrops, by our prehistoric ancestors. In Gobustan, the land is sliced through with deep ravines, or gobu in Azerbaijani, and some liken it to a "sea of rocks". The discovery of the petroglyphs in the 1930s here was a matter of pure chance. The area was being exploited for stone quarrying, when one day a worker noticed some strange paintings on a rock face. Archaeologists over the years have uncovered another six thousand such pictures, the earliest of which date back all the way to the tenth century BC.

The rock images depict humans, bulls, lions, deer, horses and many more animals, some of them life-size. Others give a valuable insight into civilisation during that time, showing labour practices, battle scenes, dancing and more.

The first place to visit upon reaching the park is the museum. The dozen or so rooms display photographs of some of the most important petroglyphs and give in-depth interpretations of the pictures. The museum also tells the story of the discovery of the petroglyphs and of the subsequent research and analysis.

A five-minute drive from the museum you enter the petroglyph reserve itself. Here you can walk through the gorges and view the petroglyphs in situ. Some are very prominent and easy to spot, whereas others might take a bit more patience to find. It is a stimulating exercise to try to decipher the meaning of each. English speaking guides are available to help you get the most out of your visit.

Mud volcanoes (Map L, Point 53)

There are around one thousand mud volcanoes in the world, and four hundred of these are in Azerbaijan. Many of these are located in the Gobustan region, just a short drive away from the petroglyph park. However, don't worry. Unlike regular volcanoes, these are not thousands of metres high spouting hot lava and ash clouds. Instead, they are like oversized molehills, about a metre or two high, and at the top of each mud slowly bubbles and plops in a pool much like a giant mud bath.

Mud volcanoes are an unmistakable sign of subterranean oil and gas deposits, which explains why there are so many in Azerbaijan. The mud originated from deep underground, where water is heated and mixed with mineral deposits. This slurry is then driven through cracks and fissures by subterranean pressure imbalances until it eventually emerges to form the volcano. On occasion, perhaps every twenty years or so, things liven up a bit with spontaneous combustion of methane gas many hundreds of metres high. Such eruptions could be the reason Zoroastrianism became such a widespread religion in these parts.

The volcanic mud appears to have medical benefits and can be used to treat central and peripheral nervous disorders and diseases of the skin and digestive tract. It is also thought to be great for younger looking skin!

When driving around this area keep a look out for wet, black patches in the desert. This is where oil is seeping unbidden out of the ground. It's not pollution but rather a natural process.

Preparing for your visit to Baku

— Essential info —

When to visit

Azerbaijan has a continental influenced climate. However, the presence of the Caspian Sea and the nearby Caucasus mountains makes the country climatically diverse, and nine out of the eleven recognised climate types are present in the country.

However, it is possible to make some generalisations for a visit to Baku. Days during spring and autumn are pleasantly fresh and crisp, with nights becoming quite chilly. During the winter, temperatures vary between around 5C to 10C, with occasional icy conditions at night. Summer is the best time to visit with warm, sunny conditions and temperatures hovering around 32C, although it may feel hotter due to high humidity.

Rainfall is relatively low, averaging five rainy days each month. However, in the summer months from May to September, rain is much more scarce.

Visas

Azerbaijan has a relatively relaxed visa regime. Almost 100 nationalities can apply for an e-visa online from the official Republic of Azerbaijan Visa Portal, evisa.gov.az. The cost is USD 20, and it takes three working days to process. Citizens of most western European countries, Gulf states, Australia, New Zealand, Japan, Korea and Singapore, can use this service. For all other nationalities, it is necessary to apply for a visa in advance at an Azerbaijani embassy.

Currency

The currency is the Azerbaijani Manat (AZN). Each Manat splits into 100 Gepik. At the time of writing, February 2018, one US Dollar bought 1.69 Manat, one British Pound bought 2.36 Manat, and one Euro got 2.08 Manat. You can easily exchange these main currencies in the city, and exchanges and banks are commonplace. ATMs also accept Visa, Visa Electron, Mastercard and Maestro cards.

Time Zone

Baku is in the Azerbaijaini Time (AZT) zone, which is GMT+4. The country does not currently observe daylight savings time.

* * *

Electricity

Azerbaijan's electricity is of the 220V/50Hz variety. The wall sockets take plugs with two round pins. Take a range of adaptors with you to make sure you can connect.

— Getting There and Away —

By Air

Baku has one airport serving all international and domestic airlines. Heydar Aliyev International Airport (GYD) is about a 20 km drive northeast of the city centre, further out on the Absheron peninsula. It is the busiest airport in Azerbaijan and the whole of the Caucasus region, with a wide range of routes spanning the Middle East, Europe, Russia and America.

Here are the airlines currently connecting **international destinations** with Baku:

- Aeroflot has daily flights to Moscow Sheremetyevo, with onward connections on its services and those of the SkyTeam Alliance. www.aeroflot.com
- Air Arabia links Baku with Sharjah daily. www.airarabia.com
- Air Astana flies to Almaty and Astana. www.airastana.com
- Azerbaijan Airlines offers the widest selection of destinations from Baku, including New York JFK, Beijing, Sharjah, Dubai, Kuwait, Baghdad, Tehran,

Istanbul, Ankara, Antalya, Tbilisi, Tel Aviv, London Heathrow, Paris, Milan, Lviv and Kiev. Russian destinations include Moscow Domedodovo, Moscow Vnukovo, St. Petersburg and Kazan. www.azal.az

- China Southern flies to Urumqi twice a week. www.csair.com
- Etihad flies to Abu Dhabi. www.etihad.com
- FlyDubai offers flights ten times a week to its Dubai hub, with onward connections around the Middle East, Africa, the Subcontinent, the Caucasus and Europe. www.flydubai.com. Alternatively, passengers can connect to Emirates' global network.
- Lufthansa has flights to both Ashgabat and Frankfurt. www.lufthansa.com
- Iran Air www.iranair.com and Mahan Air www.mahan.aero fly to Tehran, Iran.
- Iraqi Airways connects Baku to Baghdad and Najaf. www.iraqiairways.com.iq
- Israir flies to Tel Aviv twice a week. www.israir.co.il
- Jazeera Airways goes to Kuwait twice a week. www.jazeeraairways.com
- Pegas Fly has a daily flight to Moscow Zhukovsky airport www.pegasfly.ru
- Qatar Airways has double daily flights to its hub at Doha, from where you can connect to its global network. One of these daily flights also stops off at Tbilisi. www.qatarairways.com
- S7 flies to Novosibirsk and Moscow Domodedovo. www.s7.ru
- Turkish Airlines has a flight to Istanbul four times every day. From its Istanbul hub, you can fly just about anywhere in the world. www.turkishairlines.com
- Ukraine International Airlines flies to Kiev.

www.flyuia.com
- Ural Airlines flies to Yekaterinburg twice a week. www.uralairlines.com
- UT Air goes to Surgut and Moscow Vnukovo. www.utair.ru
- Uzbekistan Airlines links Tashkent to Baku. www.uzairways.com
- Wataniya links Baku with Kuwait three times a week. www.wataniyaairways.com
- Wizz Air flies to Budapest once a week. www.wizzair.com

As Azerbaijan is quite a small country, there are not too many services to other cities domestically. However, Azerbaijan Airlines flights connect the **domestic** destination of Ganja with Baku three times a week.

By Rail

There is a relatively extensive railway network in Azerbaijan, comprising almost 3000 km of track and 176 stations.

Baku is connected to several international destinations, including Moscow, Tbilisi, Kharkov and Rostov, as well as many other Russian cities.

Domestically, tracks cross pretty much the whole country, including the entire Caspian Sea coast, the southern border with Iran, and central and northwestern regions. The fare is unlikely to exceed more than USD 5 anywhere in the country.

Tickets can be purchased online on the Azerbaijan Railways website, https://ticket.ady.az/en. The site also has full timetable and route information, displayed in English.

By Road

The most straightforward route is from Tbilisi in Georgia. An overnight bus service takes about eight hours. Buses leave from the Avtovagsal bus station in the northwest of the city.

To the north, it is also possible to go by road to Russia, although current security concerns in Dagestan makes this option inadvisable. To the south, the Astara border crossing with Iran can be reached by taxi or bus in about five hours. To the west, the border with Armenia is closed.

By Boat

Baku can be reached by ferry from Turkmenbashi in Turkmenistan. The journey takes about seventeen hours, with boats leaving every day or every other day. There is also a ferry service from Aktau in Kazakhstan, a trip taking thirty hours and with departures every three to five days.

The term 'ferry' should actually translate as old, rusting cargo ship. The schedules are informal at best and are dictated by loading and by the mechanical readiness of the vessel itself. Therefore, this option is best for adventurous souls with plenty of time on their hands.

— Getting Around —

From the airport

The most convenient and cheapest way of getting to the city centre is by the Aero Express service, which operates modern 48-seater coaches. These leave every 30 minutes throughout the day, except between 9 pm and 5 am when it reverts to an hourly frequency. The journey to the 28 May metro station and central railway station takes thirty minutes and costs 1.5 AZN. Cash is not accepted on board these buses, and you need to buy a BakuCard from a kiosk in the terminal, so ensure you have some local currency available.

For taxis, follow signs for 'Official Taxis' and book with one of the marshalls. The official taxis are white London taxis, and the journey should cost 25 AZN. It is best to ignore the many men offering taxis as soon as you walk out of the terminal.

The metro does not currently serve the airport. However, from the city centre to the airport you could get a red line metro to Koroglu, where you can pick up one of the many taxis to take you to the airport for about 10 AZN.

Around the city

As explained in the detailed walking tours in this guide, the majority of sights are accessible on foot. However, for when feet get tired, or if the weather is not cooperating, the good news is that there are extensive public transport networks. These are supported by well-designed websites, available in English, with maps and routes all easily accessible to make journey planning a breeze.

The metro and bus networks operate on a cashless basis, and to use them you first need to get a BakuCard. Vending machines are at the airport, in all metro stations and at some bus stops. You can buy an extended use card for 2 Manat which you can then top up as much as you like. Alternatively, you can purchase limited use cards for between one to four journeys. All one-way rides on buses and metros, regardless of length, cost 0.20 Manat, making it one of the cheapest public transport networks in the world.

Baku's metro system operates from 6 am to midnight with trains running at a frequency of every two to three minutes. There are two lines, with the red line linking Icherisheher with Hazi Aslanaov, and the Green line connecting Khatai to Darnagul. The central interchange is 28 May station. Trains and stations are safe and clean. Listen for the pieces of music played before arrival at each station…each has been specially chosen for its relevance to that stop. For more information on the metro, visit www.metro.gov.az/en.

Baku's bus network spreads its tentacles across the entire city, out into the suburbs and across the Absheron peninsula. They can take you just about anywhere you want to go. Note that the buses no longer accept money and passengers should use the Bakucard. For full information on buses, visit www.bakubus.az/en.

Finally, you will see taxis cruising everywhere around Baku, and you can easily hail one from the street. The London taxi cabs have meters, with each kilometre costing 0.70 Manat. To hire other taxis you will need to negotiate. Perhaps the most convenient option is Uber, which now operates in the city.

— Where to stay —

Due to its oil and gas industry, and thriving economy, Baku is jammed with top-end accommodation options. However, by booking early you can still get good deals, and there are many other options at all levels. Here are just a few highlights in the top end and mid-range categories, however www.booking.com lists all the possible options at the competitive rates. Furthermore, Tripadvisor.com compares prices with the three or four top hotel consolidators, making sure you get the most reasonable rate. There is also a wide selection of apartments and rooms to rent in Baku on www.airbnb.com.

Top end

Hyatt Regency Baku is in a quiet part of Baku about a 25-minute walk from Fountain Square. Huge, comfortable rooms and excellent facilities include two 25 m swimming pools - one inside and one outside.

Fairmont Baku can be seen from all over Baku, as it's in one of the iconic Flame Towers. Facilities include six dining options, a spa, and rooftop and indoor swimming pools. You also get direct access to the Flame Towers complex, with many restaurants, bars, shops and an IMAX cinema.

Four Seasons Baku has quite possibly one of the best locations in the city, in a lavish building right on the Baku Boulevard, a stone's throw away from the Maiden Tower and Old Town. It has become the place to see and be seen in Baku and is frequented by wealthy and high profile guests.

JW Marriott Absheron is well situated next to Freedom Square and Government House, near to Baku Boulevard. There's a variety of restaurants and bars, an indoor swimming pool and on-site fitness centre.

Hilton Baku is directly across Freedom Square from the JW Marriott, handy for the main Nizami shopping street.

* * *

Mid-range

Park Inn by Radisson is just across Neftchilar Prospect from the Park Bulvar Mall. This good value option has all the facilities of its more expensive counterparts, including modern rooms, free Wi-Fi, fitness centre and good in-house dining options.

Holiday Inn Baku is in a bustling commercial and business area just east of Freedom Square. Guests rate the hotel for its modern, spacious rooms.

Qafqaz Baku City Hotel is an ultra-modern, highly-rated four-star option in a quiet area a short taxi ride away from the centre. In addition to the usual facilities, it has a sun terrace and spa with hot spring bath.

Bristol Hotel Baku is just a few steps from the Old Town in a cosy old building. Some of the double rooms come with a balcony. The hotel is one of the top-rated value for money options in Baku.

The Old Street Boutique Hotel is located right next to the Old Town city and is rated number one amongst Baku B&B and Inns on TripAdvisor. It's only got eleven rooms, so you need to book well in advance.

Index

A

Arno Babajanyan Concert Hall 126-27
Asaf Zeynali Street 224-25
Ashur mosque 224
Ateshgah Fire Temple *Baku* 265-67
Ateshgah Fire Temple *Tbilisi* 61
Azerbaijan State University of Economics 246

B

Bailov Stones 231
Baku Boulevard 260-62
Baratashvili Street 53
Bayraq 260
Berikaoba Statue 52-53
Biltmore Hotel 32
Boats *Baku* 282
Boats *Tbilisi* 106-7
Boats *Yerevan* 197
Boom Town 239
Botanical Gardens 72
Bridge of Peace 47
Bukhara caravanserai 216
Buses *Baku* 284
Buses *Tbilisi* 108
Buses *Yerevan* 198

C

Cafesjian Sculpture Gallery 132-33
Charles Aznavour House Museum 135-36
Charles Aznavour Square 147-48
Circular Park 156-57
City Hall 248
Climate *Baku* 277
Climate *Tbilisi* 101

N

O

P

Q

Copyright

FewDaysAway

PO Box 215878
  Dubai
  United Arab Emirates

This edition published 2018.

Copyright (c) Stephen Stocks 2018